THE HIGH-ALTITUDE ENTREPRENEUR

THE HIGH-ALTITUDE ENTREPRENEUR

A Framework for Scaling Smarter,
Leading Better, and Living Freer

Chris Clearfield

CERTIFIED

(H)

WRITTEN
BY HUMAN

CONTENTS

INTRODUCTION

You've built something real. A growing company, loyal clients, a reputation that means something in your market. The kind of business that was supposed to give you freedom—more choice, more time, more impact. On paper, you're a successful entrepreneur running a successful company.

But from the inside, it doesn't always feel that way.

You're hiring, scaling, improving—and still, too much depends on you. Every system you design needs tending. Every process you step away from slowly bends back toward your inbox. The team is capable, but when things break, they wait for your signal.

You've tried to systematize, to delegate, to give your team more ownership. But too often, things slip through the cracks, proving yet again that the only thing you can fully trust is yourself. You know it can't stay this way, but every attempt to step back feels like an invitation for chaos. So you keep holding on, not out of ego, but out of care—for the work, for your people, and for the fragile order that lets it all keep moving.

You're proud of how far you've come, but the business seems to run on your vigilance more than its own momentum.

That's the **low-altitude cycle**, the invisible pattern that traps so many high-performing founders. You solve problems faster than anyone else, so the business learns to depend on your speed. You push for excellence, so accountability flows only one way: up. Growth exposes new cracks in the system, and you're the one patching them.

While this seems like failure, it's actually the natural consequence of success. The same instincts that once powered your growth— like hustle, urgency, precision, control—start to create friction as the business evolves.

But this is solvable. You can break that cycle.

The next stage of growth isn't about doing more; it's about seeing more. Entrepreneurs design their businesses through repeated choices and reactions. Every check-in, every late-night fix, every "let me just handle it" teaches the organization how to behave. Over time, those choices harden into systems, and those systems produce predictable results: stalled capacity, overreliance, and fatigue.

The High-Altitude Framework™ helps you see and redesign those systems. It turns invisible habits into visible structures. It gives you the altitude to understand why things feel harder than they should and the tools to build a business that runs on more than your constant presence.

This shift isn't loud or dramatic. It's deliberate. It's the move from reaction to awareness, from firefighting to forward motion. When you operate from that altitude, freedom stops being an aspiration and becomes the natural byproduct of your ability to see the hidden patterns of your entrepreneurship.

The Moment I Saw the Pattern

I didn't build a $50M company. I didn't found a unicorn. I'm not writing this from the deck of a catamaran.

What I have done is spend years coaching the entrepreneurs who did. And from that vantage point, I noticed that success didn't always bring freedom. More often, it felt like a trap.

Though I'm an entrepreneur myself, my greatest insight didn't come from scaling my own business. It came from standing slightly outside the swirl—close enough to understand it, but far enough to see what others missed. In my training as a Gestalt coach, I learned that all behaviors have value and that real change begins when we can see the hidden value in how we're operating right now. That lens gave me a different way of noticing.

One moment stands out. I was in a group coaching session, listening to founders celebrate their wins. Revenue was up. Teams were expanding. On paper, they had "made it."

But underneath, they were still managing their own calendars, bottlenecking key decisions, and carrying that low-grade hum of anxiety that never shut off. They weren't failing, but they were trapped by the instincts, beliefs, and behaviors that had powered their growth.

And then it clicked for me: they didn't have a problem to solve. They had a hidden tension that lay beneath all of their choices.

I began helping entrepreneurs name those tensions—control vs. delegation, speed vs. thoroughness, growth vs. stability—and see what was behind them. The effect was powerful. Entrepreneurs who had felt stuck started to see their choices differently. They weren't instantly "fixed," but they could finally pause, step back, and create space for better decisions.

One of my clients, Laurel Parks, the co-founder and COO of Houston Pump & Gear, described it this way:

"Once I used the framework to name ego as the driver behind my control instinct, I could finally pause. I started spotting it in my gut reactions, my quick fixes, my need to be in the middle of everything. Naming it didn't erase the reflex overnight, but it gave me a structure for practice. For the first time, I had both the language and the lens to make better choices. And over time, that gave me real freedom."

Moments like that showed me I was onto something bigger than a coaching conversation. This wasn't about solving isolated problems. It was about giving entrepreneurs a repeatable process to uncover the hidden forces shaping their work and to practice leading from a higher altitude.

Over time, I began distilling these patterns into what is now the High-Altitude Framework™: a systematic way for founders to navigate tensions, break out of the productivity trap, and design businesses that scale with clarity and unlock entrepreneurial freedom.

The framework emerged from these relationships and observations: from watching brilliant founders shift their beliefs, release old instincts, and begin designing the kinds of businesses and lives they actually wanted.

Operating from Altitude

When founders operate from altitude, everything feels different. You start the morning without a wall of pings and interruptions. Your team's already in motion, solving problems without waiting for you to weigh in. There's white space in your calendar: time to think, to design, to ask the bigger questions that used to get crowded out by the urgent ones. You finish the day with energy left, not only because you're no longer carrying it all yourself, but because you're actually doing the work that you're great at.

Freedom looks different for everyone. For one founder, it's sitting in a café with his teenager on a Tuesday morning, laughing instead of scanning for messages. For another, it's walking onto the shop floor and realizing that her operations manager has already handled the bottleneck that would've derailed production six months ago. For others still, it's an uninterrupted afternoon of deep work, the kind that changes the trajectory of the company. These are small moments, but together they mark a profound shift: the move from vigilance to vision. This is what altitude feels like.

Businesses reliably produce what they're designed to produce. Every result, good or bad, is an expression of how the system* was built. Systems are not abstract; they're created through hundreds of micro-decisions: who gets looped in, how you respond under pressure, what you tolerate, what you reinforce. Those choices congeal into patterns, patterns into culture, and culture into the invisible machinery that drives every outcome, including the ones you don't want.

Most leaders try to fix symptoms—tweaking org charts, rewriting SOPs, or pushing harder on accountability—without realizing their system is doing exactly what it was designed to do. The leverage is upstream: seeing the design itself.

The High-Altitude Framework™ helps you do that. It surfaces the unconscious tensions, shaping your choices and makes the hidden patterns of your entrepreneurship visible so you can redesign the context of your business and reclaim agency. It's not about more effort; it's about awareness, practice, and deliberate redesign.

In the chapters ahead, you'll learn how to use the High-Altitude Framework™ step by step. You'll start by **naming your Power Tension**, the core tension that silently drives your business. This

---

* When I say "system," I don't mean a shiny piece of software or a slick project-management dashboard. A system is broader and deeper—it's the way the moving parts of your business connect, reinforce each other, and produce the outcomes they produce.

is where clarity begins: identifying the real engine behind your overwhelm so you stop solving the wrong problems. Then, you'll **map this tension**, turning seemingly opposing forces into visible structure. The map shows the competing values and hidden payoffs that shape your decisions, making it possible to see a coherent picture of your business challenges rather than a tangle of disconnected issues.

Next, you'll **create Super Choices**: clear, integrated decisions that move you out of reactions that keep you stuck. You'll turn each Super Choice into small, low-risk experiments that let you test new ways of leading in real time, building confidence and traction without disruption. Finally, you'll **catalyze ownership** with your team, translating individual leadership into collective action. You'll learn how to co-design commitments with your team, distribute accountability, and build a cadence of collaboration that allows energy and initiative to flow through the business, not just roll up to you.

This framework is practical, field-tested, and safe to try. It doesn't ask you to change who you are; it helps you see what's been driving you so you can lead with greater freedom, focus, and ease.

This is the work of generating altitude—clear, structured, and entirely within your reach.

From Awareness to Practice

Reading creates awareness. Practice creates change.

The High-Altitude Entrepreneur Workbook is where you put the ideas in this book to work, turning reflection into action and momentum.

This isn't bonus material; it's where you make progress. Each section builds on the last, laying out, step-by-step, the High-Altitude Framework™, helping you see patterns, make better choices, and lead with more ease. If you're ready to turn clarity into momentum, download the workbook at no charge here: **highaltitudeworkbook.com** or by using the QR code.

What's next

You've already done the hard part—you built something real. Now it's time to make it lighter, stronger, and freer. This book is your guide. Each chapter builds the habits, language, and systems that let you lead at altitude—with clarity instead of control, direction instead of drag.

You don't need to push harder. You just need to see differently, practice deliberately, and keep climbing.

If you're ready to lead with altitude, turn the page.

CHAPTER 1

The Stress of Low-Altitude Thinking

"There is nothing so useless as doing efficiently that which should not be done at all."
— Peter F. Drucker

Greg was halfway through movie night with his two teenage kids when his phone buzzed. It was another issue from his project manager, the kind that should have been solved two layers down but somehow still landed in his inbox. He slipped out of the room to answer the team's message, the laughter from his kids fading behind him.

The project was a dream on paper: build a massive branded entryway where a pro sports team would charge onto the field through a giant set of sculpted shark's teeth. Exactly the kind of bold, immersive work Flowstate Studios, his 25-person design/build firm was known for.

But instead of sketching new concepts or celebrating the win, Greg was triaging client requests, clarifying specs, and making calls his team was hesitant to own.

This wasn't new. For decades, his studio had produced jaw-dropping, one-of-a-kind experiences for brands and corporate clients. On paper, it was thriving—steady pipeline, impressive portfolio, even a recent rebrand to finally put his own vision at the center. But behind the scenes, cashflow was fragile. Operational gaps meant deadlines were barely held together by late nights and heroic pushes. And Greg himself was still the bottleneck, the one his team came to for approvals, fixes, or direction.

That night, he recognized an uncomfortable truth: "I spend 90% of my time on things that I was never meant to do."

Greg wasn't creating anymore. Not really. He wasn't sketching, building, or dreaming. He was firefighting, plugging leaks in budgets, answering frantic emails, stepping into HR issues, and untangling vendor snafus. Every time he tried to look up, something urgent yanked him back down.

What he really needed was to spend his time and focus moving beyond one-off builds and create a product-based marketing line his team could scale—a catalog of imaginative, modular pieces that brands could adapt for events across the country. He saw the future clearly: repeatable products that still carried the wow-factor of custom design, a revenue stream that wasn't handcuffed to the unpredictable cadence of big clients and complex installs.

The shift he envisioned would free up cashflow, stabilize the business, and finally give him back the creative oxygen he'd been suffocating without. But instead of building it, he was stuck inside late-night email threads about bolts for shark teeth and shipping logistics. Every hour he spent trapped in reactive emails was an hour stolen from that vision, and the gap between what he dreamed and what he lived only seemed to widen.

The irony was brutal. Success was supposed to create freedom. Instead, it had become a trap. His company looked strong from the outside, but it was strong because he kept holding it up. If he stopped driving, he feared the whole thing would collapse. In the meantime, the creativity that built it all was slipping away.

By the time he returned to movie night, the credits were rolling. His kids were brushing popcorn off the couch cushions, already moving on.

Greg was exhausted, frustrated, and—maybe for the first time—starting to wonder if he could keep going like this. What he couldn't yet see was that nothing accidental was happening. His business was running exactly as it had been designed— around his instincts, his urgency, and his vigilance. Every time he stepped in to save a project, he taught the system to wait for him. The company wasn't broken; it was faithfully expressing the way he led.

Low-Altitude Alert

Even if you're a successful entrepreneur, it's likely you've also felt the friction of a business that technically works, but only because you're constantly pushing. You're not alone. Many founders find themselves in a similar bind: their companies have grown, but so has the weight of keeping them running.

Let's take a closer look at why that happens.

Most entrepreneurs dream of freedom when they start their business. But somewhere along the way, that freedom gets buried under a mountain of complexity. Instead of leading, we're reacting. Instead of strategic vision, we're stuck in day-to-day firefighting. And even with a strong team, the founder still ends up being the linchpin.

You're not imagining the pressure—it's real.

And it's not just your business. It's the world around you.

We live in an era of unprecedented complexity. Geopolitical shifts are disrupting supply chains and market access. Younger employees bring new expectations that are reshaping workplace culture. Remote and hybrid models have changed how teams collaborate and blurred the boundaries of accountability. AI is rewriting entire industries at a pace few can match. All the while, regulatory pressures are tightening across the board, turning even basic leadership decisions like firing an underperforming employee into complex, high-stakes calls.

And the cost doesn't just show up in your calendar; it shows up in your body, your sleep, your relationships, and your creativity. You wake up already behind. Your mind keeps running even when you're with your family. The edge that once made you unstoppable now feels like exhaustion wearing a mask of focus.

The pressure isn't just out there in the market; it's inside the design of how you work. When complexity rises, your company starts to echo your patterns of response. If urgency is your default, your culture learns to run on urgency. If control keeps you safe, control becomes the operating system.

The Low-Altitude Experience

You're putting a lot of energy in your business, solving problems, driving progress, but it still feels like a grind. Your team gets things done, but they don't take the lead. Strategic projects drift. Long-range goals blur. Stepping back feels risky, not freeing.

You might be feeling similar to Greg in ways that are hard to name but become unmistakable once you recognize them. Let's map out how some common Low-Altitude patterns—and the tensions beneath them—might be playing out in your day-to-day.

1. You're Doing Instead of Leading

Instead of setting the direction for your business, you're constantly doing things.

Alex is a rockstar, and that's the energy he built his business with. As the guitarist for the punk band Midnight Ember and the founder and CEO of Fretwise, he thrives on speed, spontaneity, and the thrill of creating in the moment.

Fretwise is an online platform for learning guitar that interacts with nearly a third of all active guitar players in the English-speaking world.

In the early days of the business, Alex's creative hustle worked brilliantly. He was everywhere—filming ads, tweaking landing pages, answering customer emails, and rallying his team with rapid-fire decisions. The energy was electric. Problems got solved in real time.

Now, with a team of 15, things moved slower. Too slow. A simple website update that should've taken a day stretched into a week. A new promo campaign sat in limbo, caught in endless revisions. Frustrated, Alex jumps in—rewriting copy, fixing designs, and editing content.

The work gets done, but at a cost. His team's work is never quite right in his eyes. Copy's not sharp enough. The designs aren't dialed in. So Alex frequently redoes things, convinced that it's faster than creating the space for better work the first time around.

The same perfectionism that fueled Alex's success on stage and in the early days of business keeps him buried in details, constantly reworking instead of leading.

Fretwise had become a machine that depended on him. Without clear systems, stepping away felt impossible. "I created the business so I could focus on music," Alex told me, "but if I step back, the wheels fall off."

The irony is that the traits that built the business—speed, control, precision—had become its limits. Alex's habits had written themselves into the company's DNA, and the harder he worked to fix it, the deeper the pattern set in.

2. Your Team Is Misaligned

You hold the vision, but your team isn't executing it. Maybe they don't fully understand it. Maybe they resist change. Either way, they're pulling in different directions, and instead of feeling like they're supporting you, you feel like you're dragging them uphill.

Consider the example of Evan, a brilliant designer who had stumbled into a niche business—designing and building large-scale experiential installations for resorts and entertainment venues.

His business had a reputation for building the impossible, but behind the scenes, it was stuck. Growth had plateaued, and the long sales cycles, combined with the risk of last-minute client cancellations, left his team scrambling to keep projects on track. He saw the solution clearly: tighten operations and hit deadlines to preserve margins, and diversify into new revenue streams like architectural metalwork and fabrication. But his leadership team didn't share his urgency.

For years, they had been focused on keeping the core business running: getting crews to job sites, managing logistics, and keeping projects afloat. When Evan tried to change things, they resisted. They saw diversification as a distraction and tightened operations as unnecessary pressure. The stress grew, with Evan feeling like he was dragging the company forward while his team dug in their heels. Without buy-in, execution stalled.

Evan's frustration was mounting. He had spent years assembling a reliable team, but now he wondered if their comfort had become the constraint. Could he challenge them to rise? Or would protecting what he'd built mean sacrificing what it could become?

What Evan was really facing wasn't a stubborn team—it was a system faithfully expressing his own priorities. Years of rewarding reliability had created exactly that: reliability, not reinvention. The culture was doing what it had been trained to do.

3. You're the One Everyone Waits For

Some entrepreneurs escape the daily firefighting but still find themselves making all the major strategic calls. Your team isn't bringing half-baked ideas or bold bets—they wait for a green light from you. They execute but don't proactively create solutions. If growth still depends on your decisions, your vision, and your drive to move things forward, you're facing a deeper kind of constraint: the Leadership Bottleneck.

This is the hidden challenge of a successful but stagnant business. On the surface, things are running smoothly. Projects get done, clients are happy, and revenue is steady. But the truth is, you are still the engine of momentum. If you step back, decisions slow, initiatives stall, and your team defaults to execution rather than ownership.

This is precisely what frustrated Carlos, the founder of a successful commercial HVAC company based in the New York region. As Carlos's company grew, he tried to build a strong leadership team. They were experienced, competent, and loyal. Yet Carlos felt stuck.

Carlos had done everything the business books prescribed. He'd read Traction and adopted EOS, run leadership offsites, hired a coach, even introduced OKRs. On paper, he was doing everything right.

But despite all that structure, the same patterns kept reappearing: hesitation, dependency, and silence in meetings. It puzzled him until he began to see the mirror. The company wasn't just shaped by his strategies; it was shaped by his instincts. His drive to stay in control, his reflex to steady the room, and his habit of stepping in when things wobbled had quietly become the company's operating system. The business had absorbed his strengths as rules. Without meaning to, his unconscious approach had created the dependency that now held back his growth.

That's the quiet law of entrepreneurship: every system expresses the psychology of its leader. The company becomes a living reflection of what the founder rewards, tolerates, and fears. Until you can see that design, every fix just reinforces it.

So when it came to major decisions like expanding into new markets, restructuring pricing, or negotiating partnerships, Carlos's team didn't take ownership. Instead, they constantly waited for his approval. They didn't talk with each other. The moment he stepped away, things slowed down.

The biggest red flag came when Carlos took a family vacation to Portugal. While he was away, a critical deal with a large commercial contractor stalled. His sales director called him three times, unsure whether to accept minor contract changes. It was a seven-figure opportunity, and instead of problem-solving as a team, his leaders defaulted to inaction, afraid to make the wrong call.

The shift out of the Leadership Bottleneck isn't about delegation; it's about creating a leadership culture where your team thinks and acts like owners. That's what separates businesses that plateau from those that scale.

4. You Are the Operator in Chief, Not the CEO

The business is growing, but instead of focusing on strategy, you're buried in operational tasks. The complexity of managing people, technology, and evolving regulations keeps you from stepping into your role as a visionary leader.

A key supplier suddenly increases prices. A competitor launches a new product. A team member quits without notice. You, along with your team, spend your days reacting instead of finding new customers and opportunities.

Consider Rose, the co-founder of Summit Hydraulics, a company that manages predictive maintenance programs for large industrial facilities. Rose, whose story we'll explore in Chapter 4, knew every aspect of her business. She didn't need reports—she had it all in her head.

That was the problem.

The business was growing because Rose held all the pieces together. Every service call, every decision, every exception still ran through her.

During a recent meeting where she was working with her project manager to advance the company's new Enterprise Resource Planning implementation, her door opened eight times with interruptions.

"Did we expedite those sensors?"

"You know the customer who was scheduled to come by tomorrow? It turns out they're double booked and they're going to be here this afternoon. But we have that meeting with our OEM customer then. What should we do?"

"Which vendor are we using for that urgent maintenance call?"

Each time, she answered on instinct—because if she didn't, things slipped through the cracks. The pricing model, vendor relationships, service-level agreements—all of it lived in her brain. There wasn't a system because she was the system.

At any given moment, her mind was juggling a dozen open loops: Had the replacement sensors for the monitoring system arrived? Was the $6,000 invoice from their vendor reasonable? Had the invoice for last week's urgent service call been sent out—or was the approval still buried in her inbox?

She could feel the strain building. Part of her knew this wasn't sustainable, but she couldn't yet see another way.

Rose's story is an extreme example of a common founder dynamic: they genuinely want to stay connected and supportive. When they walk the floor or drop into meetings, people two or three layers down see them as the ultimate authority and start asking for help. And the founder responds, because they know the answer. The intent is caring, but every time they step in, they bypass the very leaders they've put in place. Those leaders begin to feel undermined, resentful even, but rarely say it out loud. Instead, they disengage. What looks like support from the top reads as interference from below.

And without a system that pushes authority down and holds learning in place, the business can't adapt; it can only repeat. The company's capacity rises and falls with the founder's availability. Until you build a structure that carries your clarity, you'll keep trading foresight for firefighting.

5. Your Success Feels Like a Trap

You make good money, but the stress is relentless. You work long hours, you're always on call, and you can't even complain about having a bad boss because you're the one in charge. No matter how much you achieve, it still doesn't feel like freedom.

For Greg at Flowstate Studios, the design firm introduced at the beginning of the chapter, the cost of firefighting was starting to become obvious. What took longer for him to see was how success itself had boxed him in. Growth had led to cash-flow stresses, fragile systems, the slow erosion of his creative spark, and too many missed moments with his kids.

Somehow, the numbers never seemed to add up. The pipeline was full, but cashflow was always tight—big invoices arriving late, contractor bills higher than expected, and razor-thin margins on custom work that demanded heroic effort from his team. Every project was a high-wire act.

That pressure shaped his leadership in ways he didn't like admitting. He said yes to clients he should have pushed back on. He absorbed scope changes instead of enforcing boundaries. He stayed silent in meetings where he wanted to challenge his team because the risk of losing time—or losing the project—felt too great.

The irony? Those compromises only pulled Greg further from his creative gifts, the special sauce that helped him build the business. He could see the future he wanted: repeatable products, stabilized revenue, and room to think big. But each short-term concession stole another inch of progress from that vision.

Flowstate Studios looked like a success story. In some ways, it was exactly what Greg had dreamed of building. But inside, it felt like a house of cards propped up by his constant vigilance. That's the trap of low-altitude entrepreneurship: the better you get at holding it all together, the harder it becomes to let go.

Synthesis

Across industries and personalities, the pattern repeats. Each of these founders built systems that performed exactly as designed—brilliantly efficient at keeping them in the center. What looked like operational chaos was, in truth, perfectly coherent. The business was doing precisely what their habits trained it to do.

The Low-Altitude Cycle

Behind the details, each of these stories has a similar arc—an entrepreneur, whose drive built their business, now finds themselves carrying its weight, holding everything together at the expense of the freedom they set out to create.

As I worked with entrepreneurs, I noticed that despite their success, many seemed to be trapped in a seemingly endless cycle of problem-solving. They were struggling with something in their business, and many seemed to have a fix that was right around the corner—a new hire, a new project management system, or a new sales strategy. When that supposed fix arrived, things got better—for a moment.

Then, almost inevitably, chaos and churn resumed.

The pattern wasn't random. Each time they solved one problem, they unknowingly reinforced the design that produced it. Their businesses were reliable machines, perfectly calibrated to recreate their founders' own reflexes under stress.

I got curious about what was happening and started to see a common pattern that I came to call **The Low-Altitude Cycle**.

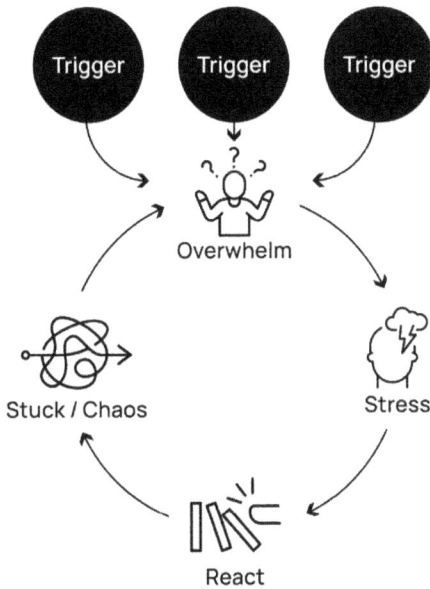

The Low-Altitude Cycle

At a fundamental level, entrepreneurs create something of value in a changing world.

Entrepreneurs make products, grow teams, find new opportunities, and improve people's lives. They create value that wasn't there before.

The act of value creation exposes them to issues they need to deal with: they need to manage team members, adjust to changing customer demand, and deal with economic and regulatory shifts.

These issues are a byproduct of success; the growth of their companies creates more complexity and consequences they need to address.

In isolation, any given issue might seem like a straightforward problem to solve. But for many of the entrepreneurs I work with, there's too much going on for us to actually solve these problems.

The totality of these issues can create a cascade of anxiety and overwhelm that triggers our stress response, which hijacks our brains and prevents us from doing our best thinking. Our ability to see the big picture narrows. And our strategic capacity collapses. (See the "In The Weeds" sidebar for the neuroscience behind this process.)

For most of us, when faced with anxiety and overwhelm, our instinct is to exit it as quickly as possible. That's when we pick up our problem-solving tools and go to work.

But because we're trying to move forward from a place of stress, we're not doing our best thinking. We're reactive, and reactive actions create more chaos. Even though it seems like we're moving forward, we're actually staying stuck.

This is the cycle—not only do the issues keep coming, but the very solutions we're trying end up creating more chaos.

At this point, what most founders miss is that their businesses mirror their own habits. The urgency, control, or perfectionism that once drove success becomes the default way of working. It's not a flaw in the business—it's a reflection of how you've learned to lead.

That's why every fix you attempt while stressed keeps the cycle alive. It's not a time problem; it's a design problem.

Once you can see that your business mirrors your inner wiring, everything changes. The problem isn't your people or your tools; it's the invisible architecture built from your habits, fears, and strengths. That's good news because what you've designed, you can redesign.

In the Weeds

Many entrepreneurs believe time is their biggest bottleneck. But time isn't the issue, attention is. The real constraint is our ability to focus on what matters most, and nothing disrupts that focus more than being "in the weeds."

Being in the weeds means getting consumed by small details or juggling so many urgent tasks that you can't step back and think strategically. When this happens, our brain enters a threat state, cutting off access to the prefrontal cortex, the part responsible for executive function and creative problem-solving.

A perfect example? A waiter on a busy shift.

I was recently at a hotel in San Diego with my parents and kids. My mom and I went to the lobby café to order smoothies. The waitress, overwhelmed with taking orders and delivering food, rushed past us several times without making eye contact.

When we finally got her attention and ordered, she sighed, "Oh, I'm out of smoothies." A beat passed before she added, "We don't have any ice."

If there's one thing mainstream American hotels have in abundance, it's ice. Practically every floor has an ice machine. My face lit up into a big smile. I love finding creative possibilities.

"Can we get you some ice?" I asked.

She hesitated, then nodded. A few minutes later, we had our smoothies.

The problem wasn't a lack of ice; it was her inability to see a simple solution because she was stuck in reactive mode.

This is exactly what happens to entrepreneurs. When you're in the weeds, working harder won't get you out. The solution isn't more time; it's better thinking. That's where the High-Altitude Framework™, introduced in Chapter 2, comes in: a new way of working that's designed to break the cycle of stress and reactivity and restore clarity.

How Does the Low-Altitude Cycle Show Up for You?

The specifics may look different—creative hustle, a misaligned team, stalled leadership, endless firefighting, or success that feels like a cage—but underneath, the same principle holds: your business reflects your patterns. It orbits around you. Your constant presence keeps it alive, but that same gravity keeps you from rising. That's the paradox of low altitude: it rewards your effort in the short term while stealing the clarity, creativity, and independence you built the business to enjoy. No matter how successful you are, the fundamental dynamics don't seem to change.

So how does this all land for you? Take a look at the following statements, shared by entrepreneurs who've lived through the same patterns. Let them be a mirror, and notice which ones you relate to:

1. "I'm running faster and harder than ever, but it's like climbing a mountain made of sand—I'm slipping back with every step."
2. "I can't keep spinning all these plates, but I don't see a way to step back without them crashing to the ground."
3. "I'm constantly trying to convince my team to think bigger, but their comfort zone feels like an anchor holding us back."
4. "I want my team to operate like a symphony, with everyone playing their part in harmony. Instead, no one listens to each other and nobody's in tune."
5. "We've outgrown our systems, but every attempt to improve things feels like adding more wires to an already tangled mess. At some point, the whole thing's gonna go up in flames."
6. "I've built a strong team, but I'm still the one people come to when it's time to make a real decision. It's not chaos, but we're not multiplying, either."
7. "I keep giving space, hoping they'll rise to it. But instead of stepping up, they wait. It's like everyone's playing it safe—and that's not how we grow."

If any of these patterns strike a chord, or if you found yourself nodding along and recognizing pieces of your own story, you're not alone. Thousands of entrepreneurs are flying at low altitude, held in cycles of stress and reactivity even while their businesses look successful on paper.

Recognizing that you're in The Low-Altitude Cycle is a real win. It means you can finally see the pattern that's been pulling you down. That awareness is the first step toward breaking free and beginning the climb.

But awareness alone won't change reality. Without a new approach, the cycle pulls you back in, no matter how clearly you see it. What you need is a path forward, a way to rise into being a High-Altitude Entrepreneur.

The climb out of the Low-Altitude Cycle begins with seeing differently. That's where we go next.

CHAPTER 2

Enter the High-Altitude Entrepreneur

"Today's problems come from yesterday's solutions."
— Peter Senge, The Fifth Discipline

I want you to meet Priya, a corporate chef-turned-entrepreneur who runs Wow! Foods, a natural foods brand that focuses on organic dips and spreads.

"After I decided to leave my position as an executive chef for a large campus operation, I knew I wanted to get back to the creativity and relationships that brought me to food in the first place.

Wow! Foods started out pretty small-scale, with a regular presence at a farmers market, and eventually a food truck. I knew we had growth potential so I started exploring a brick-and-mortar restaurant with a small, high-end store co-located inside."

Then the pandemic hit, and Priya had to make a pivot.

"We spent about nine months figuring out how to reformulate our flagship products for retail sale. Then we were off and running. We landed ourselves in our local grocery co-op. Then in a regional chain. Our marketing was great, our brand had loyal customers, and distribution and revenue were growing. It felt like we had made it through the uncertainty of the pandemic and we were off and running."

About two years after her pivot, I met Priya for the first time. She had recently landed her biggest account yet. She thought it was just the break her business needed.

But just six months later, she felt like she was holding the company together with duct tape.

Growth placed enormous demand on her operations. Her team grew by 50%. Volumes rose, which required more manufacturing space, expanded cold storage, and new suppliers.

All these moving pieces increased complexity and logistics. Spreadsheets that worked a year ago now felt laughably inadequate. Every team meeting seemed to uncover new fires to put out, except now, the flames were bigger.

Priya drove her team hard, trying to build systems at the same time they were ramping up production.

It was hard going. "Every problem we solved seemed like it created two more. It was like we were playing whack-a-mole, but the moles were winning. I found myself carrying all the stress of my job as a corporate chef without the stability, support, or salary."

Her frustration peaked one Friday night when she found that a reefer (refrigerated) truck, used for overflow storage, had been set to an incorrect temperature without anyone noticing it. As a result, Priya had to throw away tens of thousands of dollars' worth of product.

"We didn't have automated alerts. We didn't have tight tracking. We missed something we should have caught days before."

Priya wrote to me that night. "Growth was supposed to make things easier. Instead, it feels like the bigger we get, the more chaos there is to deal with."

What was keeping Priya stressed and stuck weren't the specific problems she was facing; it was how she was approaching them.

Like many entrepreneurs, Priya believed the best way to manage her growing business was to knock down problems as they appeared. More demand? Add manufacturing capacity. More volume? Lease reefer trucks. Tracking systems buckling? Buy better software.

Each move made sense on its own. She was taking decisive action—eliminating obstacles the way any strong operator would.

But the fixes didn't create relief. They created ripple effects. More overhead. More systems to manage. More people who needed direction. Every decision carried unexpected consequences no one had the time to consider.

Priya wasn't failing at execution; she was solving problems in isolation, when what she really needed was to see the whole picture. Her business wasn't breaking down because of one bad call. She was stuck in the Low-Altitude Cycle.

Her issue wasn't the software or the trucks. Those were just symptoms. The real issue was that she was using problem-solving tools to try and fix what was actually a bigger issue in how she and her whole team operated. No matter how fast she moved, problem-solving tools couldn't get her out of the hole she was in. They only dug her in deeper.

Problem Solving Creates More Problems

As we build our companies, we lead with our instincts. We double down on the strengths that made us successful in the first place— speed, precision, relationships. If we move fast, our company moves fast. If we're detail-oriented, systems stay tight. If we're relationship-driven, culture hums with trust and camaraderie.

These instincts aren't just personal; they influence the underlying way that our businesses operate. They shape how work gets done, how decisions are made, and what gets rewarded. They imprint themselves in the muscle memory of the company.

These strengths also have downsides.

When we lean toward control, for example, we build a business where every decision runs through us. That makes us the bottleneck. When we move fast, our company lurches, always chasing the next idea and never getting its feet under it. When we focus on relationships, we smooth over conflict instead of resolving it, and efficiency suffers.

That's the paradox of entrepreneurial growth. The strengths that launch us can start holding us down. We become the center of gravity: every decision, idea, and breakthrough orbits us, and nothing escapes our pull.

For seasoned entrepreneurs, the problem-solving reflex shows up in quieter ways—jumping in to accelerate a project, tweaking a proposal, or greenlighting a strategic plan. These fixes work in the moment. But over time, they teach your team to look to you instead of out to the horizon.

This is the hidden cost of founder-led strength. As founders, we shape our organizations in deep ways. So when your instincts have been responsible for growth, it's hard to notice when those same instincts start becoming a constraint.

Priya was an exceptional operator and problem solver. She powered the early growth of her brand, but that approach didn't work as her business grew.

It wasn't that she was doing something wrong; her business had entered the next stage, and her leadership needed to evolve with it.

She wasn't struggling because of failure. She was struggling because the strengths that worked so well before didn't work in her new context.

This isn't just about one founder. It's a pattern I see all the time.

At a high level, overused strengths are our weaknesses. Or, as executive coach Marshall Goldsmith puts it, "What got you here won't get you there."

Why Do We Solve Problems?

So why do so many entrepreneurs double down on problem-solving, even when it's not working?

Because it's what we know.

Problem-solving gives us a hit of accomplishment. It feels productive. And we're good at it. Our education system trains us to find answers to known questions. Our businesses reward us when we put out fires. Our clients praise us when we deliver solutions.

When the challenge is simple—fixing a broken link in a supply chain, hiring a vendor, adding a step to a process—it works.

But the deeper issues we face as entrepreneurs aren't simple. They're messy, ongoing, and interconnected. They aren't so much problems to solve as tension to manage.

Problem-solving focuses on elimination. Managing a tension requires elevation. It asks us to see a bigger picture and hold both sides of an issue so that we can navigate through.

Deeper entrepreneurial questions—like who and how we hire, how we serve our customers, how we grow, and what we identify as our core strategy—don't have simple answers. They have tradeoffs that we need to balance.

For these questions, problem-solving falls short. As MIT professor John Sterman puts it: "There are no side effects—just effects." When we treat our dynamic and interconnected business like a simple, static system, what appear to be simple solutions have broad effects. We don't just solve a problem; we trigger three more.

In the moment, Priya wasn't making irrational decisions; she was doing what had always worked. Solve fast. Push forward. Clear the path.

But as the complexity of her operations grew, each fix created new instability. Instead of building momentum, she was feeding the chaos. Her strength of decisive problem-solving was turning into her kryptonite.

The Low-Altitude Cycle Traps Us in Problem Solving

Let's look back at The Low-Altitude Cycle to understand why a strong, smart leader like Priya wasn't able to just see the challenges of her problem-solving strategies and change.

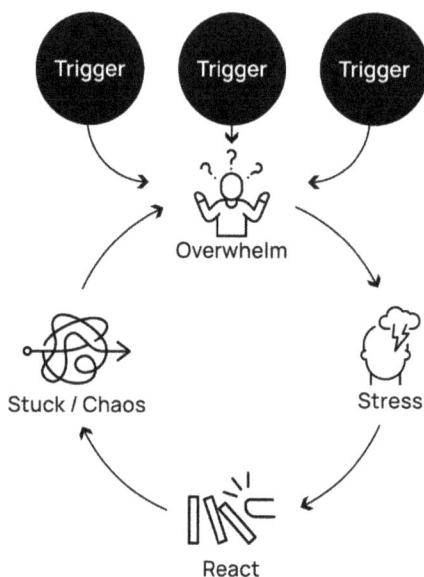

The Low-Altitude Cycle

Can you see how Priya's dynamic maps onto the cycle?

Her business wasn't breaking down from one bad move—she was stuck in a loop where stress triggered reactivity, quick fixes created churn, and clarity evaporated under the weight of urgency.

You might think that if Priya just looked at the big picture, she could change how she reacted to the issues and respond more effectively. You might expect that of yourself. Many of us feel frustrated with ourselves when we can't seem to get out of an ineffective loop. We think it's just a lack of willpower or poor systems holding us back. But this isn't a problem that Priya—or any entrepreneur—can simply think their way out of.

Even when we're committed to thinking strategically and innovatively, we often can't just pull ourselves out of the Low-Altitude Cycle.

Why? Because stress and anxiety short circuit our ability to think clearly and pull us back into old survival strategies—coping mechanisms that make us react habitually instead of responding thoughtfully.

These coping mechanisms are called conditioned tendencies** or CTs—the automatic responses we learned early in life to manage stress and keep ourselves safe.

Many of these conditioned tendencies come from what psychologists call small-t trauma: the ordinary but repeated stresses of life that shape us all. School pressures. Family expectations. A parent, teacher, or boss who made you feel you were never good enough. Some CTs come from more extraordinary circumstances—big-T trauma: major life events—abuse, loss, and violence that leave deeper imprints on the nervous system.

Whether our traumas are big or small, they create patterns of emotional and behavioral reaction that live in the body, and these patterns can resurface when we're under stress as entrepreneurs.

** The idea of "conditioned tendencies" exists in many different psychological lineages. In Gestalt, it's often referred to as behavioral responses that are "well-developed," meaning the paths that we intuitively take. I have opted to use the phrase conditioned tendencies, which I encountered for the first time at the Strozzi Institute, because I find it more accessible and intuitive.

For some entrepreneurs, their CT is control—grabbing the wheel and micromanaging. For others, it's avoidance—pulling back and hoping problems will resolve themselves. Still others default to overwork—grinding harder and trying to outpace the discomfort.

In the moment, these reactions aren't irrational, they're protective. They're incredibly smart, adaptive strategies that our bodies have internalized because, at some point in our past, they helped us feel safe, accepted, or in control. But in the present, they can sabotage collaboration, creativity, and forward progress. A quick comment made in frustration can shut down a teammate. A rush to a solution can blind us to better options. An instinct to withdraw can leave others feeling abandoned.

This is why escaping the Low-Altitude Cycle is so difficult. It's not just about bad habits or poor systems; it's that under stress, our nervous system is wired to pull us back into reactivity. Until we learn to recognize and work with those patterns, we risk building our businesses around survival instead of vision.

The antidote isn't more structure or more problem-solving; it's growing our ability to work creatively amidst stress, anxiety, and overwhelm.

That's exactly what the High-Altitude Framework™ unlocks.

The High-Altitude Framework™

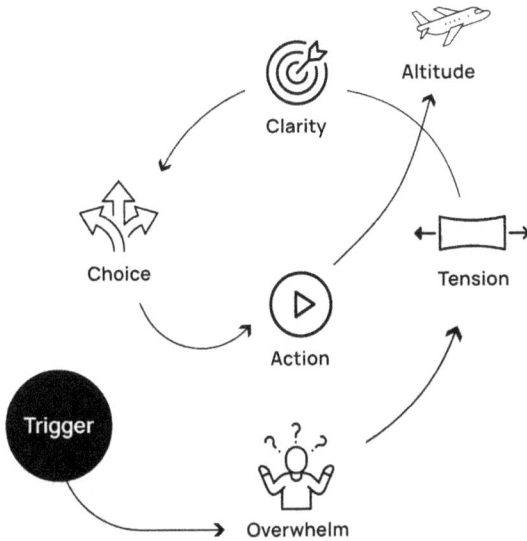

The High-Altitude Spiral

In contrast to the Low-Altitude Cycle, we have the High-Altitude Spiral, which actually starts in the same way: with a trigger and subsequent overwhelm. But from there, instead of reacting from a place of stress and creating chaos and churn, you take a step back, see the picture more clearly, and make a choice that propels your team forward.

The entry point to the High-Altitude Spiral is the High-Altitude Framework™, a powerful four-step process where you reframe the challenges in your business. Each step is designed to lift you out of reactive, low-altitude thinking and into the clarity, calm, and creativity of strategic leadership.

When you're operating using the High-Altitude Framework™, you transform how you think, how you decide, how your team collaborates, and, if you choose to, the culture of your organization.

Ultimately, it leads to freedom.

The rest of the book focuses on how you can implement this framework. Here, in brief, are the four steps that we will explore in the next chapters.

Step 1: Surface and Claim Your Power Tension
First, we identify the tensions at the heart of our overwhelm. Every entrepreneur is shaped by hidden tensions: seemingly opposing forces that pull you in different directions. The first step, which we explore in Chapter 3, is to name the one that matters most right now: your Power Tension. This gives us access to insight.

This isn't about solving a problem. It's about surfacing the invisible push and pull at the heart of your current stuckness. Once named, your Power Tension becomes a compass that brings clarity to confusion, direction to drift, and language to conversations that otherwise stall.

Instead of getting bogged-down in the stress of the Low-Altitude cycle, you use curiosity to unearth the tension you're caught in.

Step 2: Create Clarity with a Tension Map
With your Power Tension named, the next step is to map it. Using a simple 2x2 framework, you'll chart the upsides and downsides of each side of the tension. This powerful Tension Map short-circuits

our unconscious biases and helps us build a complete picture of where we are.

When you have mapped your tension, you see why your current patterns persist and how each "side" has helped you succeed so far. This removes judgment, invites curiosity, and grows your understanding. From that understanding, you'll spot the real opportunities for change.

Seeing the whole picture helps shift us out of the Low-Altitude Cycle. Instead of being pushed toward reactivity to resolve stress, we are able to step back and see the whole picture.

Step 3: Create Super Choices

Instead of swinging from one extreme to another—control to chaos, growth to burnout—Chapter 5 shows you how to use your map to design Super Choices: smart, strategic moves that honor both sides of your Power Tension. What makes these choices "super" is that they combine the best, most powerful aspects of each side of our tension. They are possibility made real. These aren't compromises. They're creative integrations.

Super Choices unlock forward momentum by capturing the best of both worlds and avoiding the stress and churn of the Low-Altitude Cycle. They create transparency and foster shared ownership. This makes the next action feel obvious, collaborative, and possible.

Step 4: Catalyze Ownership

You can't scale what only lives in your head. The final step is to bring your team into the process, not through top-down decisions, but by inviting co-ownership. We convert Super Choices into catalysts by enrolling our team in whatever comes next.

Chapter 6 shows you how to use the framework to structure honest, energizing conversations that build alignment, spark initiative, and relieve pressure from your shoulders. Instead of pushing the business forward alone, you'll create lift from within.

Taken as a whole, the High-Altitude Framework™ creates momentum so you can escape the Low-Altitude Cycle. You'll stop solving the same kinds of problems over and over. You'll learn to spot your own patterns and to avoid being "hooked" by them. And you'll expand into the ease and growth that is at the heart of entrepreneurial freedom.

At higher altitudes, the triggers don't disappear, but your relationship to them transforms. The strengths you once leaned on under stress—working harder, seizing control, pushing through—no longer run the show. You begin to shed those survival strategies where they've outlived their usefulness, while still drawing on them when they truly serve you.

For your team, this shift is just as liberating. They're no longer shaped by your conditioned tendencies, trying to match your pace or adapt to your instinctive moves. Instead, you open space for them to bring their own strengths forward. Overwhelm becomes a spark for collective clarity, not just another round of firefighting.

Taking the Next Step

When we met Priya, she was carrying a business that had outgrown her way of leading. The instincts that once fueled her growth—speed, grit, decisive problem solving—were now keeping her trapped in the same exhausting loop she needed to escape.

If that feels familiar, it's because every entrepreneur who grows past sheer hustle eventually hits this wall. You can't push your way out of it. The harder you drive, the more the Low-Altitude Cycle tightens around you.

Priya's story isn't just hers; it's a mirror. The firefighting, the spreadsheets that no longer work, the late-night worries about whether the company depends too much on you—that's the Low-Altitude Cycle. If you've felt it, you already know it won't let go on its own.

The way out isn't more effort. It's a shift in perspective. The moment you see the cycle for what it is—a loop powered by fear, urgency, and old habits—you begin to rise. Freedom stops being something you hope for someday, and becomes a choice you can make now.

That's exactly what the High-Altitude Framework™ is designed to help you do. Not quick fixes. Not tactics for a certain kind of company. A way of thinking and leading that works no matter your industry or stage.

In the next chapters, you'll see how other founders use the framework to break free. You'll also find step-by-step instructions embedded in each chapter designed to apply the method to your own business. And, if you're committed to turning clarity into momentum and you haven't already done so, you can download The High-Altitude Entrepreneur Workbook at: highaltitudeworkbook.com or use the QR code.

When Priya returns later in the book, you'll see what happened when she finally stepped out of the Low-Altitude Cycle and into a new way of leading.

The climb to entrepreneurial freedom starts here.

CHAPTER 3

Step 1 – Surface and Claim your Power Tension

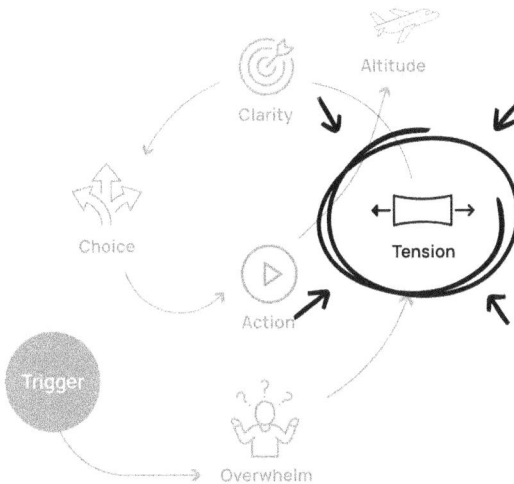

The High-Altitude Spiral: Tension

"Paradoxical thinking requires that we embrace a view of the world in which opposites are joined, so that we can see the world clearly and see it whole."

— Parker Palmer

Jim's Story

Jim is a contractor-turned-entrepreneur who runs a high-end residential construction and remodeling business, Legacy HomeWorks. Jim grew up in Spokane, Washington and studied engineering at the University of Washington. During the summers, he worked on framing and remodel crews to put himself through school, hauling lumber, swinging a hammer, and learning the rhythm of job sites. After he graduated, he worked for a year as an engineer at a major aerospace company. The pay was steady, but most of his days were spent in meetings and paperwork.

"I got into engineering because I loved building stuff. But almost immediately I realized that the work of a junior engineer at a big aerospace company wasn't for me."

So he quit and moved back to Spokane. He went back to construction, picking up work with small remodel crews, where every day was a crash course in juggling subs, and solving problems with whatever was in the truck. He learned not just the craft, but also how to work efficiently and manage the inevitable surprises of a job site.

On weekends and after hours, he started taking on side jobs—kitchen remodels, decks, basement finishes—for friends and referrals. Nights and weekends weren't enough anymore, and he realized he needed to start pricing his work properly and putting real contracts in place.

That's when he made it official, filing the paperwork, hiring subs directly, and founding Legacy Homeworks so he could take on larger projects that required coordinating electricians, plumbers, and finish carpenters instead of just swinging a hammer himself.

In the past decade, Legacy Homeworks has grown to be one of the preeminent contractors in the greater Spokane, Washington area, and they've recently expanded to Coeur d'Alene, Idaho. At the same time, Jim and his wife started a family, a change that made the 70-hour hustle weeks he once pulled on job sites impossible. Growth meant new pressures at work and new responsibilities at home.

These days, Jim is constantly pulled into conflicts between his project managers—focused on keeping budgets and schedules intact—and his site supervisors, who are battling delays, material shortages, and clients changing tile selections at the last minute. When they can't agree, the decision lands on his desk.

"I never wanted to be the tie-breaker," Jim says, "but somehow, that's where I've ended up."

Instead of thinking about strategy or focusing on design, he's stuck fielding urgent calls and site visits, just to keep things moving.

"My inbox and phone are filled with urgent questions that steal my focus. On any given day, I'll get texts like:

- City pushed the electrical inspection again. Do we eat the delay or shuffle subs?
- Cabinet lead times just got extended six weeks. Do we order a temp set or stall the project?

- We're still waiting on the Daugherty final payment. You want me to press harder?"

Jim's in the weeds. And that has real consequences.

Rushed projects lead to time-consuming rework—like drywall getting patched twice or cabinets being pulled and reset—and delays are just as bad: both frustrate clients and eat into margins.

Jim and his team are burning out. Managers feel powerless, and job superintendents feel unheard.

"We're all wiped out. I can't keep running the business this way."

For Jim, it's not just about the company. He wants to be present for his family, to coach his kids' teams and sit at the dinner table without constantly thinking about his to-do list.

He was enveloped in the turbulence of the Low-Altitude Cycle.

This chapter is focused on how exploring tensions helped Jim escape the cycle. But first, what is a tension?

What Is a Tension?

A **tension**, in the sense that we're using it, is a dynamic between two opposing but valuable forces***. Neither side is "right" or "wrong." Both bring something useful, and both have downsides when overused.

You've probably experienced some of these tensions before:

- **Control vs. Delegation** – Stay in control and things go your way. But over-control and you choke your team's growth. Delegate skillfully and you create leverage in your organization. Over-delegate and you create chaos.
- **Speed vs. Thoroughness** – Move fast and you get momentum. But move too fast and quality suffers. Embrace thoroughness and you avoid rework and quality problems. But if you're too thorough, nothing ever gets done.
- **Stability vs. Innovation** – Stay stable and protect what's working. But too much stability kills the spark that made you successful. Innovate well and you grow your portfolio of offerings; over-innovate and you're chasing shiny objects and diluting focus.

There aren't single solutions for these tensions. They're forces to navigate and continually balance.

*** For many entrepreneurs, tensions are synonymous with disagreement, and they try to minimize them. We don't like tensions within our leadership team. We don't like it when there's tension between different parts of our organization or disagreements with partners or subcontractors. We find this kind of tension uncomfortable, and so we either avoid it or try to get people to "play nice." That's different from what we're talking about here.

What I have seen with the entrepreneurs I have worked with is that tensions live just beneath the surface of their biggest leadership and business challenges. Once you start seeing the world through the lens of tensions, you realize that the work of leadership isn't about eliminating one side in favor of a quick fix. It's about learning to embrace the best aspects of both.

Exploration Equals Altitude

When we're in the Low-Altitude cycle, our stress spikes and our bodies go into survival mode. The mind narrows. Urgency takes over. We grip harder at problems, chasing quick fixes that only create more chaos. It's reactivity on repeat.

Exploring a tension interrupts your stress response. Instead of scrambling for a solution, you pause long enough to get curious about what's happening behind the scenes. This single shift—away from "fix the problem" toward "see the whole picture"—is what begins to pull you out of survival mode.

Curiosity is the engine of this shift. In the stress state, your nervous system is braced for threat. But when you lean into curiosity, your body relaxes. The tightness in your chest softens. Your mind expands. Instead of feeling trapped in urgency, you reclaim your agency. You're not being tossed around anymore; you're navigating.

This is why it's so powerful to explore the tensions in your leadership and your business. It invites you to notice the deeper dynamics shaping your overwhelm. Beneath every fire drill or bottleneck lives a tension. Once you glimpse it, the complexity that once felt suffocating begins to soften its grip.

This seems simple, and probably like something you already know. Of course exploring your options is key to effective decision making. So why, if we know this, do so many entrepreneurs continue making snap decisions that create more chaos and complexity? Often it's because we don't know we're in a stress response. As we've seen, reactivity feels like a strength.

The key is to recognize that exploration isn't passive; it's active leadership. It's the kind of action that doesn't feed the frenzy. You're not playing whack-a-mole; you're seeing the pattern. By doing less of what your stress demands, you create space for more of what leadership requires.

Ask the Tension Question

In my work with entrepreneurs, I've found that the most effective way to start exploring tension is through a deceptively simple tool I call the Tension Question. When you're about to make a problem-solving move, whether you feel stressed or not, ask:

What are the seemingly opposing forces at play here?

This question sounds straightforward, but it does something profound: it disrupts the stress reflex that keeps us trapped in reactivity. Instead of lunging for the nearest solution, our attention shifts outward. The mind opens. The field of vision widens. We start to notice dynamics we couldn't see amidst the press of urgency.

The Tension Question is deliberately plural. Rarely is a challenge shaped by just one force. Complexity arises because multiple forces are always interacting, often beneath the surface. By naming them, even clumsily at first, we reclaim agency. We stop being yanked around by problems and begin to see the bigger game we're in.

Here's the real shift: the goal isn't to find the "right" answer. In fact, chasing tidy answers pulls us back into problem-solving mode. The power of the Tension Question is that it reorients us toward curiosity. Each possible force you name is an opening, not a conclusion. Simply naming them loosens the grip of stress and primes your brain for creativity.

The moment you ask the Tension Question, you're no longer operating at low altitude. You've lifted above the churn, liberated from the narrowness of firefighting. Problems stop looking like isolated emergencies. They become part of a broader landscape of tensions—forces to be managed, not moles to be whacked.

This is exactly what happened with Jim. Once he started asking the Tension Question, he began to see the stress of his daily disputes in a new light. What felt like endless site-level squabbles revealed the deeper tensions shaping his whole business.

Jim Asks the Tension Question

Before Jim explored the Tension Question, he shared how it felt amidst all the juggling he was doing.

I feel stressed all the time. My brain is buzzing and I never have time to think—I'm just chasing whatever fire is in front of me. It's this mix of movement and feeling stuck, like 'If I don't jump in right now, this whole thing is going to fall apart.'

I'm impatient because moving quickly seems like the only way to survive. My project managers and site supervisors feel it. I'll either bark quick decisions just to keep things moving, or I'll step in and start solving details they should be handling. It's not that I want to micromanage, but I feel like I don't have a choice.

The kicker is that while I'm putting out one fire, I'm already bracing for the next. It's exhausting, and even though I'm 'doing' a lot, I don't feel in control. It feels like the business is running me, not the other way around.

That was the backdrop as we started asking the Tension Question: What are the seemingly opposing forces at play here?

At first, Jim named a long list, more than half a dozen different pulls on his attention. Together we honed them. The result was a clearer set of tensions shaping his leadership challenge:

- **Speed vs. Quality** – the pressure to move fast without cutting corners
- **Control vs. Delegation** – holding the reins tightly while needing others to step up
- **Growth vs. Stability** – chasing expansion without losing what already works
- **Revenue vs. Profit** – pushing top-line sales while safeguarding margins

- **Business vs. Lifestyle** – building the company while wanting space for family and life outside of it.

These weren't tidy answers. They were the contours of the real game Jim was in.

As Jim saw them laid out, something shifted. His voice slowed. He leaned back in his chair. For the first time in months, he wasn't just firefighting, he was naming the bigger forces at play. Simply surfacing these tensions gave him a sense of relief. Instead of being yanked around by chaos, he could see the pattern. And in that clarity, he felt a spark of agency return.

Tensions are Universal

What Jim uncovered isn't unique to him. In fact, the tensions he named are ones I hear from entrepreneurs across industries and stages of growth. That's the point: while the specifics differ, the underlying push and pull is nearly universal. I've found it's helpful for entrepreneurs to see the kinds of tensions that show up most often. This isn't about picking one from a list—it's about recognizing familiar patterns and gaining language for what you're already navigating.

Identifying a **useful tension** (see the sidebar) isn't always straightforward. It can be tempting to describe challenges in black-and-white terms: this is good, that is bad; this works, that doesn't.

But useful tensions don't live in the black-and-white. They emerge where both sides offer something valuable, and where the goal isn't to eliminate one side, but to find a more integrated way forward.

Useful Tensions

When entrepreneurs start using the lens of tension, they can unconsciously weaponize the practice to avoid shifting out of their conditioned tendencies—the habitual reactions that can guide decision making.

For example, let's say you have always leaned to perfectionism. In a discussion with your team, you might present "Careful/Sloppy" as a tension to consider.

That's not a useful tension because it comes pre-loaded with a judgment: "careful" is good, "sloppy" is bad. You can tell it's not a useful tension because you would use the word "or" to combine these forces instead of "and." Useful tensions elevate the and. Test it out: try labeling something "careful and sloppy." It doesn't work.

A useful tension is one where both sides offer something valuable. Your goal isn't to eliminate one side, but to create a new way forward that embraces the best of both.

Contrast careful/sloppy with speed/thoroughness. We get a hint that speed/thoroughness is a powerful tension because it balances the emotional "flavor" of each extreme. There are situations in your business that call for speed and those that call for thoroughness.

When entrepreneurs and leadership teams start thinking in terms of useful tensions, conversations shift. Instead of debating whether to move faster or get more precise, they begin identifying which areas require speed and which demand thoroughness. It's not just better decision making; it's better shared ownership.

In many cases, you're not dealing with just one tension; you're navigating three or four layered on top of each other. That's okay. In fact, that's normal. Strategic leadership often means holding multiple tensions in view at the same time: short-term revenue vs. long-term brand, centralized efficiency vs. decentralized ownership, innovation vs. standardization. It's less about solving one clean puzzle and more about building a way of working that holds space for multiple forces, so your team can see clearly and act wisely.

When you start to orient around tensions, it's not about landing on the "right" tension—it's about exploring and seeing what resonates. It's about putting pen to paper and experimenting, so you can stop swinging between overcorrections and start seeing a truer picture of what your business is actually navigating. That's when real progress becomes possible.

And you don't have to start with a blank slate. Over time, I've noticed that entrepreneurs are often facing a common set of tensions. Let's look at some crucial tensions to see how they shape entrepreneurs in different ways. (See Appendix A for a more complete list.)

Tension: Control vs. Delegation

In the early days, control is necessary. You have to do everything because there's no one else. But as your team grows, that same instinct becomes a hidden limiter. You stay involved longer than you should. You become the decision-making hub. And even when you delegate the task, you hold onto the decision.

Entrepreneurs like Jim often don't resist delegation outright. They want their teams to step up. They've tried to empower people. But what keeps them stuck is that when they step back, quality slips—and worse, clients notice. So they stay half in, half out.

They hand over authority, but not ownership. They offer responsibility, but without the context or support that makes good decisions possible. At the first sign of trouble, they revert to control. Instead of empowering others, they develop the dependency they were trying to avoid.

The result is a slow, creeping burnout for both the entrepreneur and the team.

This tension isn't resolved by letting go completely. It's resolved by creating clear context around expectations, decision rights, and ownership so that delegation doesn't mean losing control; it means building others' capacity and judgment.

When done well, it multiplies your leadership capacity and gives your team the room to grow. When you avoid delegation, you become the ceiling of your own business.

Tension: Speed vs. Quality

Speed is how most entrepreneurs get started, and how many of them win. It's the instinct to move first, ship early, and figure things out on the fly. That reflex can be a superpower in the early stages of a business. But as the business grows, so do the stakes. Speed without quality creates rework, frustrated clients, and missed opportunities to build trust. Over time, it becomes clear that moving fast isn't the same as moving well.

For more seasoned entrepreneurs, the challenge often isn't that the business is too slow; it's that speed becomes reactive. Teams know how to hit deadlines, but not always how to deliver excellence. They rush to close loops, but overlook details. When this happens repeatedly, founders find themselves stepping back in—not because they want to micromanage, but because they're worried about what will get missed if they don't.

This is where systems become essential. Building the right systems doesn't mean slowing everything down; it means embedding quality into how the business runs. A well-designed process with clear success conditions allows your team to move quickly and get it right the first time. It reduces rework, increases consistency, and gives you confidence that excellence doesn't rely on your direct oversight. Over time, this is what creates real velocity—speed that's sustainable because quality is baked in.

Tension: Standardization vs. Customization

For some businesses, standardization is the goal. It's how you scale, streamline, and protect margins. But for creative and technical service businesses—especially those that do high-touch, one-off work—standardization can feel like a trap. The more you systematize, the more you risk dulling your edge. The more flexible you stay, the more your systems start to fray.

When your work demands flexibility, systems don't have to get in the way; they just have to be designed to support the kind of work you want to do. When your team knows where to flex and where to hold the line, you don't just protect your edge—you scale it.

Tension: Identity vs. Evolution

At a certain point, the challenge isn't whether your business can grow; it's whether you're willing to evolve with it. For seasoned entrepreneurs, the business is often an extension of your identity. It was built on your values, vision, and decisions. But that same sense of ownership can become a subtle limiter because evolving the business—scaling the team, shifting the model, and stepping back from the center—often requires evolving your role, your style, and even how you think about your value.

It's not about fixing a process; it's about letting go of an identity that's worked for a long time.

Maybe you've been the driver. The fixer. The creative engine. Maybe your team, your clients, and your reputation all depend on that. But now, the business needs something different from you. It needs space for others to lead. It needs a structure that doesn't revolve around your energy. That shift can feel disorienting, not because you don't know what to do, but because it forces the question: Who am I, if I'm not doing what I've always done?

The answer isn't to disappear; it's to evolve and step into a new kind of leadership that's less about control and more about context. It's less about driving and more about designing an environment where others can drive well. Identity doesn't have to be fixed. In fact, the most successful leaders are the ones who keep updating who they are, so the business can keep becoming what it's capable of.

Now is the moment to pause and go deeper. I designed The High-Altitude Entrepreneur Workbook with structured prompts and step-by-step exercises to support you to surface the unconscious tensions at the core of your business and your leadership.

Download it at highaltitudeworkbook.com or scan the QR code.

Focusing on Your Power Tension Uncovers Your Core Challenge

After you've surfaced the tensions in play, it's time to focus on the tension that matters most: your Power Tension.

There are two criteria that let you know you're attending to your Power Tension.

1. Your Power Tension is within your control

First, you have the freedom to move on your Power Tension.

Some tensions are created by external forces, like market dynamics, regulation, or how you work with suppliers. These may be important, but unless you can make shifts in your leadership or within your business to work with them differently, these forces can't make up your Power Tension.

Here's what happens when you orient around a Power Tension:

- **For yourself:** Stress eases, because you're no longer wrestling a dozen fronts at once. You feel calm and in charge, even when conditions are complex.
- **For your team:** Priorities click into place. Instead of scattered energy, people align around the real shift that moves the business.
- **For your business:** Progress accelerates. Addressing the right constraint creates leverage: your investments in people, systems, or strategy start paying back faster, because they're no longer stuck behind the bottleneck. Revenue *and* margin grow.

2. Your Power Tension is central to your current challenge

Second, your Power Tension is central to your current challenge. It is the constraint that governs how progress flows—or stalls—through your business. Until you focus your energy here, tackling other challenges is just problem solving in disguise.

Effort is finite. Every improvement takes time, attention, and capacity—whether it's redesigning a process, shifting your leadership approach, or changing how your team thinks about the business. Spread that effort across too many areas, and you end up tired without moving meaningfully forward.

Entrepreneurs who fail to surface their Power Tension often make changes that don't stick. They tweak systems, implement new tools, or push harder on their team, all without addressing the deeper dynamics at play. Like a rubber band, things snap back to the way they were once they place their attention somewhere else.

When you name your Power Tension, you concentrate effort where it counts. It's like finding the slowest component in an assembly line. Fixing that point doesn't just make one step easier; it frees the whole system. You generate more flow with less strain.

Naming your Power Tension doesn't solve everything overnight, but it does give you a clear point of leverage. Once you shift that point, other "problems" begin to dissolve or reframe themselves as symptoms of the larger constraint.

Jim Claims His Power Tension

Speed vs. Quality, Growth vs. Stability, Revenue vs. Profit: these were all real forces shaping Jim's business.

As we talked about Jim's list of tensions, one stood out above the rest. When he asked, "What is central to my challenge?" and "Where do I have the most room to move?", **control vs. delegation** stood out.

It met both tests.

First, it was within his control: Jim couldn't rewrite the economy or erase the complexity of custom construction, but he could shift how he designed authority, ownership, and trust inside his company. That was leverage only he could create.

Second, it was central: the reason he was exhausted, his team was frustrated, and projects kept stalling wasn't that he didn't care enough or wasn't working hard enough. It was that he hadn't yet found a way to let go of control without being paralyzed by the fear that quality would slip and everything would fall apart. Until he addressed this, no system or hire would change the underlying dynamic.

Jim realized that the real constraint at Legacy Homeworks wasn't the pace of growth or the balance sheet. It was his leadership.

Jim's continual leaning into control explained why every decision, dispute, and detail still landed on his desk. By shifting within his Power Tension, Jim could ease decision-making bottlenecks, reduce his personal overwhelm, and set his team up to grow without him needing to make every decision.

Naming this Power Tension changed the game. Instead of chasing scattered problems, Jim now had a compass. He could see how his exhaustion wasn't random; it was the predictable outcome of over-reliance on control. That recognition alone brought relief.

By naming **control vs. delegation** as his Power Tension, Jim had identified the real lever of change. He wasn't free from the challenge, but he was no longer trapped inside it. This shift—from firefighting problems to orienting around a Power Tension—gave him visibility into his own role propagating his challenge. That awareness shifted him back into choice so he could take control of what he needed to elevate out of the weeds and into altitude.

From here, progress no longer required solving a dozen problems at once. It just required working on his Power Tension. By concentrating his attention, Jim could start to see the whole picture shift to a better balance of control vs. delegation and lead his company to the next level.

Surfacing and Claiming Your Power Tension Elevates You as an Entrepreneur

Exploring your Power Tension isn't just a clever exercise; it's the first decisive act of escaping the Low-Altitude Cycle. Remember what we saw in Chapter 2: stress pulls us into survival mode. The body braces. The mind narrows. We grip harder, chasing fixes that only create more churn. That's the Low-Altitude Cycle.

Naming your Power Tension frees you from the Low-Altitude Cycle. Why? Because surfacing it does more than reveal opposing forces; it shows you the central challenge shaping your business and confirms that it's within your sphere of choice. You stop reacting to scattered problems and begin to see the deeper dynamic at the core.

That recognition calms the system. Overwhelm shifts from being a threat to being a signal, pointing you toward where real leverage lies. This is the moment where agency returns. By naming your

Power Tension, you step out of firefighting and into altitude, working at the level that truly changes the game.

With your Power Tension surfaced, you now hold a compass. The next step is to put it on the map. In Chapter 4, I'll show you how to create a Tension Map, a deceptively simple tool that transforms scattered complexity into a picture you and your team can actually work with. This is where clarity sharpens, choices expand, and the climb to high altitude truly begins.

CHAPTER 4

Step 2 — Create Clarity with a Tension Map

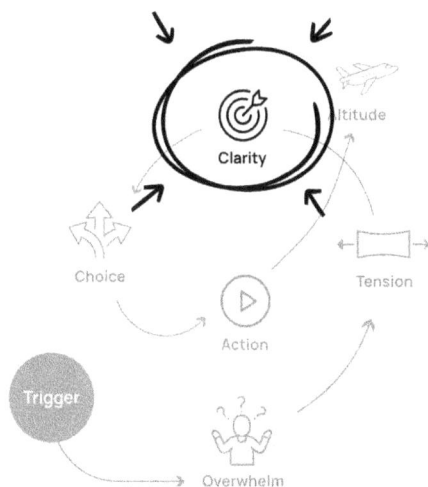

The High-Altitude Spiral: Clarity

"The test of a first-rate intelligence is the ability to hold two opposed ideas in the mind at the same time, and still retain the ability to function."

— F. Scott Fitzgerald

Rose's Story

Rose, who we met briefly in Chapter 1, runs Summit Hydraulics, a fast-growing company that manages predictive maintenance programs and digital upgrades for industrial facilities. She's not an engineer herself—her business partner is the hands-on technical lead—but Rose came up through operations and logistics, where she built a reputation as an expeditor and fixer. She carried that skill set into the company, earning trust from clients who know that if something starts to wobble, Rose's team can get ahead of it before it fails.

On paper, the company is thriving. They've secured retrofit and service contracts, expanded into IoT-based monitoring systems, and grown their team of field technicians. But behind the scenes, Rose has found herself caught in a cycle she can't sustain.

"I feel like I'm the only system in the business, but I'm not a system. I'm just one person, and everything still runs through me."

Her days are a blur of interruptions: field calls about breakdowns, procurement questions, budget approvals, staffing issues, and client escalations. She describes approving a last-minute sensor replacement order that doubled their costs, or being pulled into reconciling competing priorities between analytics and field operations. "I end up with piles on my desk, twenty things in my head, and no traction on the work that actually moves us forward."

The result is exhaustion and fear. Fear that a mistake will slip through, fear that letting go will cost too much, and fear that the entire business is still too fragile to run without her.

Yet Rose knows she wants something different. The company has grown, but she hasn't gained altitude. When she does carve out space to think, she lights up around system design: codifying workflows, creating client dashboards, and building processes that let her team act without constant escalation.

That glimpse of what's possible is what drives her forward.

For Rose, her turning point came when she named her core Power Tension: Urgency vs. Strategic Focus. She could see it in black and white. Her whiteboard was covered with strategic projects that mattered: implementing an Enterprise Resource Planning system, building partnerships, diversifying revenue. But when she asked herself how much time she had spent on any of those projects in the past week, she had to admit: less than an hour. Urgency was always winning.

"The outcomes I'm trying to avoid," she said, "I'm actually creating by holding so much. If I don't change this, the way I'm running the business will burn me out and hold the company back."

Rose's story shows how even a successful entrepreneur can get stuck in the Low-Altitude Cycle, trapped by urgency, unable to step into the kind of leadership the business really needs. Naming her Power Tension—and then mapping it—became the first step toward shifting that pattern.

Later in this chapter, we'll see how a Tension Map helped Rose create clarity and start to rebalance her focus. But first, let's step back and define: what is a Tension Map?

What Is a Tension Map?

A Tension Map is a simple but powerful thinking tool that turns invisible dynamics into something you can actually see. Once you've named your Power Tension, the map helps you lay it out on paper so you can work with it directly instead of perseverating.

The structure is straightforward: a two-by-two grid. On one side of the tension, you map the upsides and downsides. On the other, you do the same. If your Power Tension is delegation vs. control, that means writing down:

- The benefits of control: quality assurance, fewer costly mistakes, client trust.
- The costs of delegation: errors, inconsistent outcomes, risk to reputation.
- The benefits of delegation: team ownership, scalability, faster progress.
- The costs of control: bottlenecking, slowed growth, constant founder stress.

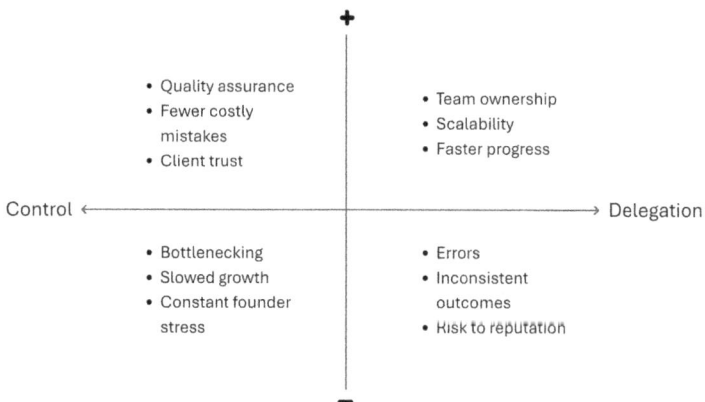

At first glance, this might seem obvious. But in practice, entrepreneurs rarely give themselves permission to see the whole picture. We tend to live on one side of the tension, clinging to the benefits of control while being keenly aware of the downsides of delegation.

The Tension Map forces a pause. It acknowledges that both sides of the tension bring value, and both carry risk. That recognition alone interrupts the instinct to operate exclusively with one opposing force.

How a Tension Map Creates Clarity

The Low-Altitude Cycle crowds out the big picture. Under stress, the brain simplifies. We make fast moves that seem obvious, but those "solutions" are built on an incomplete picture. And incomplete pictures are what drag us back into turbulence.

A Tension Map breaks that loop. By laying out both the advantages and the costs of each side, you see why your current patterns have been so sticky. You also surface opportunities that weren't visible before. The map doesn't hand you an answer, but it does expand your perspective. It creates space between stimulus and response—space where more creative, integrated choices can emerge.

This isn't about slowing down for the sake of it. It's about slowing down just enough to see clearly. When you're anchored in a fuller view of reality, that clarity allows you to move forward with confidence that's grounded, rather than being pulled into reactivity.

From Concept to Practice

The Tension Map also grounds you in the present. It asks you to start where you are—to recognize the current reality with all its upsides and downsides. That means acknowledging the value you've gotten from your default way of operating, even as you see how it's holding you back. Without that recognition, change is fragile. With it, you create a stable platform for growth.

Take Jim, for example. In the last chapter, we saw how he recognized his Power Tension as control vs. delegation. Control had been essential for him: it helped him build his business and ensure quality. But it also left him overloaded and reactive, stuck as the bottleneck. Delegation offered the possibility of scale, but only if he could face the risks and costs it carried. By mapping the tension, Jim could see both sides clearly, not as a battle of good versus bad, but as two forces that had to be worked with consciously.

That same process applies to any Power Tension. In the next section, we'll look at how Rose used a Tension Map to work with her own Power Tension: Urgency vs. Strategic Focus.

Neuroscience of Open Loops: Why Your Brain Won't Let Go

In the 1920s, psychologist Bluma Zeigarnik made a fascinating discovery: unfinished tasks stick in our brains far more than completed ones. This phenomenon, now known as the Zeigarnik Effect, explains why we keep replaying unresolved problems, why cliffhangers hook us into binge-watching, and why open loops demand our mental energy even when we want to move on.

When entrepreneurs face complex challenges, their brains often default to problem-solving mode, seeking closure by resolving uncertainty as quickly as possible. But when issues are interconnected—like balancing profitability and investment or speed and quality—there's no single "right" answer. The brain perceives this as an open loop, keeping us locked in stress and limiting our ability to think strategically.

A Tension Map works not by forcing premature solutions, but by making the whole picture visible. Neuroscience shows that reframing our challenges helps us re-activate our prefrontal cortex, the part of the brain responsible for insight, creativity, and executive function.

By mapping out both sides of a tension—its upsides, downsides, and trade-offs—we close the mental loop, not by eliminating uncertainty, but by making it manageable. Instead of fighting ambiguity, we transform it into clarity. With clarity comes the space to think, innovate, and move forward with intention.

Rose's Tension Map

When Rose first mapped her Power Tension, the effect was immediate. She already sensed that Strategic Focus vs. Urgency was at the core of her leadership, but seeing it mapped out made the dynamic unmistakable.

On the urgency side, the benefits were obvious: fast response times, client loyalty, revenue from emergency jobs. But right next to them were the costs she had been living with—exhaustion, stalled systems, and a team that never got out of reaction mode.

Across the grid, the benefits of strategic focus were just as clear: stability, scalable systems, sustainable growth. The costs sat beside them too: missed opportunities, slower response, the risk of disappointing clients.

Her Tension Map looked like this:

"It wasn't some fuzzy sense anymore," Rose said. "I could see the whole picture at once. Both sides mattered. Both sides had value. But I was only ever living inside urgency."

That recognition shifted her state. Instead of carrying urgency as a constant, unspoken weight, she could finally hold it at arm's length. "As soon as I mapped it, the pressure in my chest eased. I thought: I don't have to keep spinning this blur in my head. I can work with it directly."

The map didn't erase the tension, but it changed her relationship to it. Strategic focus was no longer a pipe dream pushed aside by daily fires. Urgency was no longer an unexamined reflex. They became two forces she could balance consciously.

The more Rose looked at the map, the more she realized it wasn't just her tension. It was the whole company's. The entire business had been built around urgency—it's what made them indispensable to clients and fueled their growth. But that also came with costs: a team stretched thin, processes delayed, systems perpetually postponed.

Mapping the tension gave Rose language for something she had always felt but never fully seen: urgency has been her engine, but without strategic focus, it's also her ceiling.

Mapping Your Tension Propels You Out of the Low-Altitude Cycle

If you're in a Low-Altitude Cycle, it may feel like doing a Tension Map is obvious, or too simple to change these patterns that have become entrenched in your business. But often it's the simple things that can grow our capacity to make great decisions.

Remember Conditioned Tendencies from Chapter 2? CTs are the automatic strategies we create in response to trauma to help us feel safe, capable, or in control when facing stress. The key word here is "automatic." They may have served us well before, but when we operate from them unconsciously as entrepreneurs, they end up trapping us.

For Rose, urgency wasn't just part of her Power Tension—it was her CT. Whenever she felt pressure, she automatically moved faster, responded immediately, and solved problems herself. She couldn't opt for strategic focus when urgency automatically and unconsciously compelled her toward doing things that could have been handled by an assistant: approving invoices line by line, jumping into scheduling conflicts, even booking her own travel to avoid errors.

CTs are the mechanisms that unconsciously keep us tuned to the upsides of our dominant mode and the downsides of the opposite. They blind us to the costs that we're paying now and the benefits we might get by shifting. They don't just shape what we do; they shape what we see.

For Rose, her reactive moves weren't irrational. Urgency preserved responsiveness and reinforced client loyalty. It made her and her company indispensable. What she couldn't see was that it also kept her from recognizing the value of slowing down to build systems, partnerships, and sustainable growth. That kept her from her bigger, higher-value goals.

That's why mapping her tension was so powerful. Seeing urgency and strategic focus side by side disrupted the trance of the CT. Suddenly, she could choose—moment by moment—whether urgency was worth the cost of sidelining strategy. That pause was the first step in interrupting her CT and reclaiming her agency. For the first time, she felt like she was in the driver's seat instead of being a victim of the dynamic that had previously trapped her.

The shift didn't just matter for Rose; it mattered for the business.

Her tendency had long been mirrored by the company itself: everything postponed in favor of the urgent, strategic investments consistently sidelined. That posture was expensive. For example, rather than pulling from inventory, they were constantly ordering new parts, resulting in overstock.

When expensive specialty tools broke or went missing, the company would simply buy another, rather than invest in systems to prevent loss and theft. The default to urgency meant money was constantly spent patching problems rather than preventing them.

Once Rose began to step out of the grip of urgency, she started to prioritize long-term relationships with OEMs, key suppliers, and subcontractors. Those conversations opened up strategic solutions that had always been available but had never been seen.

One example: her relationship with a tool vendor led to an off-the-shelf tool management system. It was free for her, easy to implement, and it saved her company hundreds of thousands of dollars a year. That solution had never even cracked her top five priorities when urgency dominated. Awareness made it visible.

The lesson is simple but profound. Conditioned tendencies don't just run our behavior; they run our businesses. They shape what we notice, what we ignore, and what choices feel possible. The first step to change is awareness. When we can see differently, we can act differently. And when the entrepreneur shifts, the business shifts with them.

Map Your Power Tension

Now it's time to map.

Grab a blank page and draw a 2x2 grid. This will help you explore your Power Tension—not as a problem to solve, but as a set of forces to understand.

Step 1 - Label the seemingly opposing forces of your Power Tension

Write your Power Tension on the horizontal axis, putting the side you naturally lean toward on the left of the diagram (and if you're not sure which that is, just pick one to start). For example, put Control on the left and Delegation on the right. Then label the vertical axis with + on the top and - on the bottom (or, if you prefer, "Upside" and "Downside").

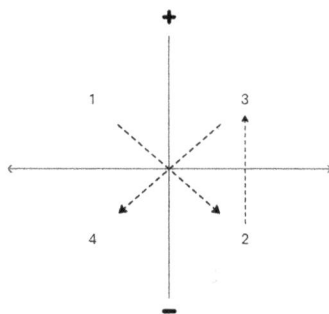

Resource

You can sketch this out yourself or download a printable version of *The High-Altitude Entrepreneur Workbook* and refer to Worksheet #4.

Download at No Charge Here: highaltitudeworkbook. com or scan the QR code.

Step 2: Start with an Upside
Begin in the top left, the quadrant labeled 1. Spend around 90 seconds listing all the positives you get from operating on this side of the Power Tension.

Step 3: Map the Opposite Downside
Now look at Quadrant 2, the *downside* of leaning into the **opposite** side of your Power Tension. Spend 90 seconds listing the costs of operating this way.

Step 4: Move to the Remaining Upside
Move to Quadrant 3 and spend about 90 seconds listing the benefits you get by operating this way.

Step 5: Complete the Final Downside
Finally, spend 90 seconds mapping Quadrant 4 to list all the costs of operating this way.

Step 6: Step Back and Reflect
Take a look at how the seemingly opposing tensions are playing out in your business. What do you notice?

From Clarity to Creativity

In the Low-Altitude Cycle, it's easy to confuse constant motion with progress—answering calls, fixing emergencies, and chasing down details. Awareness interrupts that cycle. It's the moment an entrepreneur steps back and sees the pattern: the solutions they've been clinging to are what fuels the chaos.

When you name your Power Tension and map it, you create relief and clarity. Instead of holding a blur of competing pressures in your head, you can see the whole picture on paper. Both sides matter. Both sides have value. That recognition alone interrupts conditioned tendencies that used to run on autopilot. What once felt like an endless loop of stress becomes something you grow bigger than and can see clearly.

This is why mapping is such an essential practice. Awareness isn't optional—it's the foundation. Without awareness, any attempt at change is fragile, and you're easily pulled back into unconscious patterns. With awareness, new possibilities emerge. You now have the ability to pause, to catch yourself before reacting, and to ask better questions. The choices in front of you don't feel predetermined anymore. They feel workable.

Awareness alone doesn't build the future. It sets the stage for the next step: transforming clarity into creativity. That's where Super Choices come in. A Super Choice is a high-leverage decision that integrates opposing forces instead of treating them as either/or trade-offs. Instead of asking, "Do I protect quality or move faster?" you learn to design moves that elevate both. Super Choices are integrative, high-leverage, and transformational. They reveal options that once seemed impossible and turn them into practical next steps you can act on immediately.

This is the moment when leadership shifts. You're no longer stuck firefighting between urgent demands. You're leading from a higher altitude, seeing beyond the binary and creating momentum that unlocks energy across your business.

You've named your Power Tension and mapped it. Now you're ready to move from clarity to creativity—and discover how to make the kind of choices that transform not just your role, but the trajectory of your company.

CHAPTER 5

Step 3 – Create Super Choices

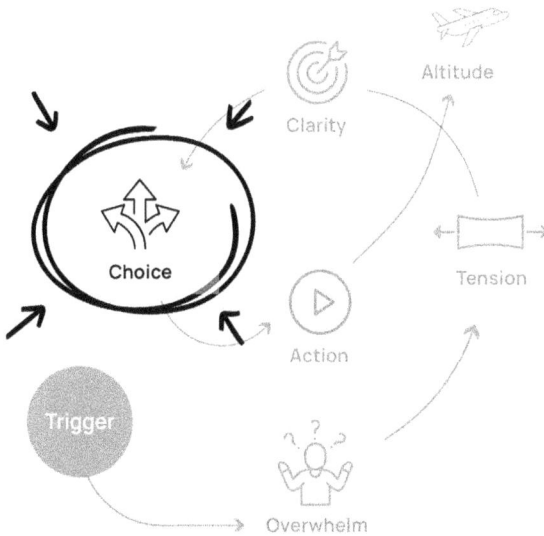

The High-Altitude Spiral: Choice

"Strategy is and will always be about making choices."
— Roger L. Martin Strategy & Integrative Thinking[1]

Andrew's Story

Andrew grew up in South Florida. His family didn't have much, and he saw early how unstable housing shaped people's lives: neighbors cycling through run-down apartments, families living in unsafe conditions, friends ashamed to bring people home. For Andrew, housing wasn't just about property, it was about dignity. He carried that conviction with him into his career.

At LX Equity, a property management firm, Andrew started on the front lines, handling tenant calls, late-night emergencies, and lease paperwork. It was demanding work, but Andrew had the ability to connect with owners and tenants alike, and had an instinct for fixing broken processes. When something was chaotic, he could make it flow.

The founder of LX Equity noticed. While others focused only on today's crisis, Andrew kept finding ways to prevent tomorrow's. He built trust with clients, defused tenant conflicts, and tightened systems that had been costing the firm time and money. Within a few years, he'd risen through the ranks, taking on bigger portfolios while building relationships with investors and developers across the region.

As growth accelerated, the firm expanded across South Florida, taking on more properties and managing larger client portfolios. Andrew thrived on the challenge, and eventually he bought out the firm's founder.

These days, Andrew finds himself stuck in a frustrating loop. A senior property manager drops the ball and an important client email goes unanswered, a monthly report is late, or a tenant concern lingers too long. The situation escalates, and Andrew has to come in "over the top."

"I don't find out about dropped balls until there's a crisis," Andrew says. "By then, I'm not coaching. I'm firefighting."

It's the same pattern every time: Andrew clamps down on authority because autonomy has failed him. But the tighter he grabs the wheel, the less space his managers have to grow. Each rescue feels necessary in the moment, but ultimately digs the hole deeper. The more Andrew steps in, the more dependent the business becomes and the less capable his team feels without him.

The irony is that every time he steps in, it works. He salvages the situation, reassures the client, and sometimes even wins more business. But each "save" carries a hidden cost. His staff feel second-guessed because Andrew only shows up when something goes wrong. His trust in them erodes, so he holds on even tighter.

Short-term wins. Long-term exhaustion. A business that looks successful from the outside but traps its leader on the inside.

That's the paradox: the instinct that built Andrew's reputation— taking control, stepping in, protecting clients—is now the same instinct that keeps the company locked in firefighting mode.

This is the reason he can't yet step into the future he actually wants. Andrew's bigger vision is to build a service arm that supports other property managers, helping them modernize and scale with the tools and processes he's refined. But he can't move forward while he's still consumed by operational chaos and constantly pulled back into the firefighting loop.

Andrew is caught in the turbulence of the Low-Altitude Cycle. The way out isn't another heroic save; it's creating Super Choices.

What Are Super Choices? Why Do They Matter?

Every business is a system. The uncomfortable truth is that your system is already working exactly as designed. If your inbox is flooded with client complaints, if deadlines are slipping, if your team hesitates to take ownership—those outcomes are not accidents. They're the result of unconscious design choices: the defaults, habits, and conditioned tendencies that shape how work gets done.

Your Tension Map captures this dynamic: the upsides you value and the downsides you fear quietly drive how the system gets built.

Take Andrew. As much as he says he doesn't want to be involved in every problem, the way he navigates authority and autonomy produces precisely that outcome. His tendencies are baked into how his business works. The same is true for every leader: beneath the stated goals, the system reflects the choices and biases that, if made unconsciously, feel safest in the moment.

Awareness is the foundation of growth. But even with awareness, I have seen that most entrepreneurs slide back into their conditioned tendencies unless they change the context that surrounds them.

When entrepreneurs stop at awareness, when they map their tensions but try to fix them alone, they end up reinforcing the patterns they mean to change. Insight without new structure doesn't create freedom; it breeds fatigue. You may see the loops clearly, but you still react the same way under pressure by tightening control, jumping back into the weeds, convincing yourself you're "just being responsible." The business keeps demanding your presence because nothing in the system has changed to make it safe for others to lead.

As you overfunction, your team follows suit. They sense the awareness but not the redesign, so they retreat to what's familiar: waiting for direction, protecting turf, and avoiding risk. Progress stalls under the weight of good intentions.

This is where the Super Choice comes in. Super Choices emerge from a focused design process that draws on the clarity of your Tension Map to let you reshape the context your business is operating in.

A Super Choice does this by considering both sides of your Power Tension[2]. Instead of defaulting to either/or trade-offs, a Super Choice leverages tension to create a way forward that captures the upsides, minimizes the downsides, and generates momentum across your system. Super Choices are integrative, transformational, and practical. They don't remain as lofty aspirations; they take the form of concrete next moves and testable experiments that stretch both leader and team into new, more effective patterns.

Super Choices not only change how you lead, they shape how your whole business operates. They prevent the cycle of firefighting by embedding intentional design into daily execution.

With Super Choices in place, entrepreneurs stop swinging between extremes. Instead of waiting for the perfect hire or the ideal conditions, they discover they can experiment their way forward and gain clarity, creativity, and momentum in the process.

This is how entrepreneurs exit the Low-Altitude Cycle. Not by muscling through more heroic effort, but by stepping into their true role: not just as the fixer of problems, but as the designer of a better future.

To step into that role, you need a clear process. Super Choices can feel abstract at first, so in this chapter we'll break them down into practical moves you can follow. And, along the way, we'll follow Andrew as he integrates Super Choices into his business.

Andrew's Tension Map

At the center of Andrew's leadership struggles was his Power Tension: Authority vs. Autonomy. On the authority side, he knew the benefits well. When he kept his hands firmly on the wheel, nothing slipped through the cracks. He could spot deviations quickly, step in, and make the right call. He trusted himself completely. But the costs were obvious: endless firefighting, too many cancelled date nights with his wife and the creeping sense that the business couldn't function without him.

On the autonomy side, the upsides were just as clear. If his team took real ownership—moving work forward and making meaningful decisions—Andrew could reclaim the space he needed to think strategically. LX Equity could move faster, innovate more, and build a culture where people supported one another instead of leaning on him. The fear, of course, was that giving too much rope meant running straight off a cliff.

At first, the choice seemed binary: authority or autonomy. But mapping the tension opened up a new line of thought. Maybe autonomy didn't have to mean taking himself out of the captain's chair. Maybe trust didn't have to be blind. What if he could design a system that held both sides, where he still had clarity and confidence, while his managers had the room to lead?

Instead of swinging between extremes, Andrew began to see the possibility of a new way forward. A path that honored both authority and autonomy without collapsing into the costs of either.

+

- High consistent quality
- Can de-escalate problems
- Feel in control

- Team has real ownership
- Can think strategically
- Things move faster

Authority ← ———————————————————— → Autonomy

- Constant firefighting
- Overwhelm & overload
- Business depends on me

- Risk of bad decisions
- Quality suffers
- Feel out of control

−

This is the essence of a Super Choice. It doesn't erase the tension—you can't erase it. But it turns the tension into a design challenge. The unconscious instinct is to solve your way from the past. The high-altitude shift is to experiment your way into the future.

Create Your Super Choice

Here's the path we'll follow to build a Super Choice:

Step 1. Use Your Tension Map to Identify Your Core Constraints.
Start by naming the real boundaries that define your playing field. Use your Tension Map to clarify the crucial upsides your next move must deliver and the disastrous downsides it must avoid. These constraints transform vague tensions into a clear design challenge.

Step 2. Generate Possibility.
Once your boundaries are clear, shift from problem-fixing to possibility generation. Turn your paired constraints

into How Might We…? questions that hold the seemingly opposing forces of the tension, and use them to spark fresh ideas that could integrate what previously felt like trade-offs.

Step 3. Sketch a Solution.
Choose one possibility that excites you and turn it into a lightweight design using the People, Process, Technology, and Knowledge framework. Sketch how this new way of working could take shape across your system. Then test it against the filter question, What would have to be true for this to work?

Step 4. Make It Real.
Translate your sketch into action through experimentation. Follow the sequence Make it work. Make it right. Make it scale. Start small, learn fast, refine what works, and only then codify it for consistency and growth. This is how a Super Choice moves from concept to transformation.

Step 1: Use Your Tension Map to Identify Your Core Constraints

Every Super Choice begins with a boundary. It's tempting to treat decision-making as if the possibilities are limitless, but in reality, they aren't. A good decision is not about chasing every option; it's about working within the real constraints that define your situation. Without those constraints, you end up with either wishful thinking or endless compromise. Constraints aren't restrictions; they are the shape of the playing field. They mark the lines between what will strengthen your business and what erodes it.

The simplest way to define those lines is through two guiding questions:

- What are the crucial upsides this choice must deliver?
- What are the disastrous downsides it must avoid?

Put differently, what success outcomes are non-negotiable, and what risks are intolerable? Together, these two questions cut through noise and help you see what truly matters.

This is where the Tension Map becomes more than just a thought exercise. Once you've plotted the upsides and downsides of each pole, you can translate that picture into non-negotiables.

Look at the downside quadrants first: which risks would sink the business if they materialized? Those are the costs you cannot afford to pay.

Then look at the upside quadrants: which benefits are so vital that the decision isn't worth making without them? Those are the gains you must lock in.

Taken together, these become the boundaries of your Super Choice.

Using your tension map to identify your constraints transforms the overlapping and interconnected considerations into a defined design challenge. Instead of bouncing between authority and autonomy, or control and freedom, you now have a set of criteria that keep you tethered to what actually matters. It's no longer about guessing at balance; it's about building within boundaries.

This is the heart of the practice. The point isn't to chase perfection or eliminate tension; it's to establish the musts and must-nots that ensure your next move strengthens rather than weakens the system. When you know your constraints, you stop designing in the dark. You stop swinging between extremes. You begin, instead, to build systems that are grounded, durable, and capable of carrying your business forward.

When entrepreneurs do this exercise, it's common for two distinct kinds of constraints to emerge. The first is a **solution constraint**: What business objectives does this need to meet?

The second is a **leadership constraint**: How do you need to show up as a leader to create the outcomes you want to create?

The High-Altitude Entrepreneur Workbook offers a detailed guide for identifying your core constraints. If you haven't already, visit: **highaltitudeworkbook.com** or scan the QR code to download.

Andrew Defines His Core Constraints

For Andrew, whose Power Tension was Authority vs. Autonomy, this step was clarifying. He had been stuck in a loop: clamping down whenever something slipped, then loosening his grip in hopes his team would step up, only to be burned again. Mapping the tension was useful, but it wasn't until he drew out the constraints that things started to shift.

Andrew's non-negotiables came into sharp relief:

- **Nothing crucial slips through the cracks** – he could not afford to lose client trust by missing critical emails, regulatory deadlines, or priority service requests.
- **Autonomy must come with visibility** – he wanted his managers to take ownership, but he knew that he still needed to build trust. So he wanted to be able to spot issues before they escalated so he could work through them collaboratively rather than reacting.
- **Responsiveness is non-negotiable** – clients needed to feel supported in real time, no matter who was handling the interaction.
- **Decisions must be truly owned** – managers couldn't simply escalate problems upward; they needed to carry decisions to completion and be accountable for both the action and its outcome.

By writing these out, Andrew started to walk a new path. He no longer saw authority and autonomy as a binary choice; he saw them as poles that needed to be held together within these boundaries. His non-negotiables became the guardrails for designing his Super Choice.

With his **solution constraint,** Andrew declared that client responsiveness is non-negotiable. Owners must feel supported in real time, whether Andrew personally intervenes or not.

The **leadership constraint** is equally important: Andrew needs accountability without micromanagement. He can't simply clamp down every time something goes wrong, because that keeps his team dependent and his inbox overloaded.

With these constraints identified, Andrew is ready to generate possibility.

Step 2: Generate Possibility

Since your business is producing exactly what it was designed to produce, if you're not happy with the outcomes, you don't need to work harder; you need to generate a new way of working.

Instead of asking, "How do I fix what's broken?" you begin to ask, "What could we create that doesn't yet exist?" That is the essence of the How Might We Question (HMWQ).

It looks deceptively simple:

How might we... ?

Don't underestimate it. This question is the heart of design thinking, and it works because it opens the door to possibility.

"How" signals that there are multiple answers, not a single right one. "Might" introduces flexibility and experimentation. "We" makes it collective rather than solitary.

When you're in the Low-Altitude Cycle, your brain defaults to firefighting questions: How do I get this client off my back? How do I stop the bleeding? How do I make sure this never happens again? Those questions shrink your options. They drag you into the weeds of reactivity.

By contrast, an HMWQ reframes the tension into a design challenge. It doesn't assume that there is an answer, it assumes there are many possibilities, and your job is to generate them.

Let's ground this in an example. Suppose your Power Tension is Client Satisfaction vs. Boundaries. On one side, the upsides of client satisfaction are obvious: referral growth, stronger brand reputation, happy clients. But the downside is equally clear: burnout, dilution of focus, and sliding profitability. On the other side, strong boundaries create predictability, clear expectations, and healthier work-life balance. But too much rigidity leads to limited service availability, constrained growth, and the risk of underserving clients.

This isn't a puzzle you can solve once and for all. Both poles matter, and both come with trade-offs. That's why this tension is such fertile ground for a Super Choice.

Here are some ways the Power Tension can be reformulated into How Might We Questions:

- How might we deliver a premium client experience while keeping the scope of work crystal clear?
- How might we avoid employee burnout while continuing to strengthen our brand reputation?
- How might we be highly responsive to clients while limiting our work to what we do best?
- How might we ensure great service without my personal involvement in every client issue?

Notice what's happening here. Each question explicitly holds both poles of the tension. You're not choosing between client satisfaction or boundaries; you're asking how both can coexist in a stronger, more creative design.

From these questions, distinct possibilities begin to emerge. For example:

- Create a tiered service model, where premium response times are reserved for top-tier clients while standard clients get reliable, predictable support.
- Introduce a "client fit filter," saying yes only to the work that aligns with your core competency, and confidently referring out the rest.
- Establish a rotating "client success lead" role among managers, so no single person, including you, is the bottleneck for responsiveness.
- Automate common service updates, freeing human attention for the moments that matter most.

- Redesign client onboarding so expectations and limits are explicit up front, strengthening trust instead of eroding it later.

Some of these are tactical. Others are more strategic. That's the point: the HMWQ creates room for both. It surfaces fresh possibilities you would never see if you were stuck trying to fix the last fire.

Now, here's the invitation: look at your own Power Tension Map and the constraints you generated in the last section. What paired constraints matter most? How might you mix them together?

Then reformulate them into How Might We Questions. Don't overthink it; just write two or three. Then, without editing yourself, start listing possible answers. You'll notice that the act of asking differently unlocks new ways forward.

If you want a more step-by-step exercise, you'll find one in the workbook. But for now, pause and ask yourself: What's your How Might We Question? What fresh possibilities open up if you stop firefighting and start designing?

Andrew Translates His Core Constraints Into Two How Might We Questions:

- How might we guarantee client responsiveness without Andrew needing to be the backstop?
- How might we ensure accountability while giving Andrew visibility, so he can coach before a crisis instead of firefighting after it?

Notice the shift. Instead of circling endlessly between two unsatisfying options—delegate more and risk disappointment, or clamp down harder and smother his team—Andrew now had design challenges that opened the door to new solutions. These questions pointed directly to system redesign.

Once he framed the problem this way, possibilities multiplied. One option was to move client communications into a centralized ticketing system with clear response-time expectations. That way, nothing slipped through the cracks, and Andrew could see the flow of requests without being the bottleneck. Another was to establish a tiered escalation pathway, so most issues were resolved at the frontline and only a few predefined situations ever rose to his desk.

He also considered shifting the team's rhythm. A weekly accountability huddle could surface red flags early, giving Andrew line of sight before small slips became big crises. On the client side, a real-time dashboard could provide owners with instant transparency into property performance, reducing their reliance on email replies for reassurance.

Other ideas emerged as well: creating rotating "on-call" roles among senior staff to spread client coverage, drafting a service-level agreement that set both promises and limits, and redesigning onboarding so clients clearly understood how responsiveness worked at LX Equity from day one. Each of these possibilities carried different trade-offs, but together they represented something Andrew hadn't felt in a long time: choice.

That was the breakthrough. None of these ideas required Andrew to work harder or his managers to suddenly become flawless. Instead, they offered a path to re-engineer the business so that accountability, responsiveness, and visibility were built into the way it operated.

This is the power of reframing with How Might We Questions. By holding both sides of his tension in view, Andrew opened the door to solutions that previously weren't even on the table. What felt like an impossible loop turned into a set of real options.

Step 3: Sketch a Solution

By now, you've seen how a well-formed How Might We Question cracks open new possibilities. But possibility on its own doesn't change your business. Ideas only matter if they get shaped into designs that shift how the system works.

Remember that every business, including yours, is a system. The outcomes you're experiencing today aren't random; they're the sum of how the system has been designed, whether through conscious choices or conditioned tendencies. Profit, growth, and client satisfaction emerge from that design. So do stress, churn, and constant firefighting—even if you'd rather they didn't.

Mike Fisher, CEO of MyFitnessPal and co-author of The Art of Scalability[3], offers a simple but powerful way to see the levers inside that system that I've adapted for entrepreneurs: **People, Process, Technology, and Knowledge.** Those four elements interact to create everything you experience. Change one in isolation and you'll usually be disappointed. Replace a tool without fixing the workflow, or shift a process without retraining people, and you'll get the same results in a shinier package. The real change comes when all four are considered together.

That's why we think of this next step not as a master plan, but as a **sketch**. A sketch is fast, lightweight, and easy to test. It's not meant to be perfect; it's meant to be good enough for now and safe enough to try. When you design sketches with all four elements in mind, you create changes that actually stick.

Let's ground this in the **Client Satisfaction vs. Boundaries** tension. On one hand, you want to delight clients, exceed expectations, and generate referrals. On the other, you know that without boundaries, you end up exhausted, resentful, and stretched too thin.

One sketch that addresses this tension is deceptively simple: **redesign client onboarding so expectations and limits are explicit up front.**

Think about how this plays out across the system.

- **People:** Your account managers are trained to confidently walk new clients through what's included, what isn't, and how communication works. They're supported to hold the line, instead of left guessing or bending under pressure.
- **Process:** A standardized onboarding sequence ensures nothing gets missed. Every client gets the same clarity from day one.

- **Technology:** Automated welcome messages, shared project dashboards, or templated FAQs reinforce what was promised in conversation.
- **Knowledge:** The core agreements—what you do, how fast you respond, and what falls outside scope—are codified and accessible, not stuck in your head.

Notice what's happening here. You're not making a binary choice between client satisfaction and firm boundaries. You're designing a system that lets both breathe: clients feel taken care of, and your team has a clear frame to deliver inside.

Everyday Super Choices

Not every Super Choice needs to redefine strategy or rebuild a system. Some of the most powerful ones operate in the everyday rhythm of leadership: small, intentional redesigns that prevent familiar tensions from turning into recurring frustration. These daily Super Choices don't require sweeping change; they require sharper awareness of the patterns that keep the founder at the center, and the courage to redesign those patterns in simple, visible ways.

One example is the tension between autonomy and alignment. The trap is to delegate work without context, assuming ownership will drive results. It rarely does. When approached as a Super Choice, you can develop a lightweight way to share context and clearly articulate goals while leaving execution details to your team. This approach preserves autonomy while ensuring the work still points toward what matters most.

The tension between your accessibility and focus follows a similar pattern. The trap is to stay endlessly available for interruptions, scattering attention and training the team to wait for answers. The Super Choice is to design clear rhythms for both availability and deep work—creating a culture where responsiveness coexists with reflection, and your attention is used intentionally, not reactively.

A third tension lives between innovation and consistency. The trap is to either chase every new idea or overprotect the current system. The Super Choice is to create a defined space for experimentation: small, time-bound trials that keep learning alive without destabilizing operations. Stability and adaptation both get to breathe.

Each of these examples shares the same architecture: a recurring tension, a predictable trap, and a simple redesign that allows both sides to coexist productively. They're small enough to implement this week but powerful enough to shift a system over time. Freedom isn't found in eliminating tension, but in learning to design from it.

Test the Sketch

Now that you've sketched the solution, you need to test it. This is where a second design tool comes in: the question What would have to be true for this to work? Popularized by Roger Martin in his book *Playing to Win*[4], it's a deceptively simple filter.

Instead of jumping straight into action, you pause and surface the hidden conditions. What assumptions does this idea rely on? What dependencies or dealbreakers could derail it? By asking this up front, you avoid wishful thinking and give your idea a fighting chance.

Here's the key shift: when you ask What would have to be true?, the answer doesn't need to see the gaps as barriers. As Roger Martin points out, those gaps may be your biggest opportunities. By making true tomorrow what isn't true today, you can turn what looks like an obstacle into the opening for your next level of growth.

Take our onboarding redesign example. For it to work, several things would have to be true:

- The team must actually use the new process, not revert to improvisation.
- Expectations must be framed in client-friendly language so they build trust, not defensiveness.
- Accountability must be clear—if a step gets skipped, who owns the fix?
- The system must evolve as needs change, with regular reviews built in.

None of these are small, but none are impossible. The beauty of surfacing them early is that you can design around them, instead of being blindsided later.

This is the difference between ideas that fade and Super Choices that last. A Super Choice isn't a reactive fix. It's a high-leverage design, anchored in your Power Tension, sketched through the system, and tested against the reality of what must be true. That's what makes it transformational.

Now it's your turn. Look back at the How Might We Questions you generated. Choose one possibility that excites you. Use the people, process, technology, and knowledge framework to see how it might land in your business.

Then ask: What would have to be true for this to work? Write down the conditions. See which ones feel doable, which ones feel like stretch goals, and which ones reveal a need to adjust the idea.

Don't aim for perfection. Aim for progress. The point of a Super Choice is not to erase the tension, but to reshape the system so it works for you instead of against you.

Andrew Sketches His Solution

When Andrew looked at the possibilities he generated, one resonated deeply with him: move client communications into a centralized ticketing system with clear response-time expectations.

Through the **people lens**, it shifted who carried responsibility. Instead of Andrew swooping in after the fact, senior managers would own the flow of tickets, each one traceable back to a clear owner. Accountability wouldn't be vague; it would be visible.

On the **process side**, the chaos of scattered inboxes would give way to a structured path. Every client message entered the same stream, prioritized by urgency, and routed with preset escalation rules. Instead of crises appearing suddenly on Andrew's desk, he could see patterns emerging earlier, when they were still manageable.

The **technology** itself acted as an enabler, not a savior. A central hub replaced the roulette of individual inboxes. Requests were time-stamped, visible across the team, and searchable by client. No more wondering who had seen what, or whether an urgent issue was lost in a thread.

Finally, the **knowledge dimension** tied it together. Service standards were codified into the system: response-time expectations, escalation protocols, and client commitments were written down, not assumed. The firm's promises to clients were no longer trapped in Andrew's head; they were visible, shared, and enforceable.

Of course, a sketch is only as good as its grounding. For this idea to work, a few things would have to be true. The team would need to actually use the system, rather than reverting to old habits. Response-time commitments would need to be realistic, framed in client-friendly language that built trust instead of overpromising. Ownership of tickets would have to be unambiguous, so nothing slipped through the cracks. And Andrew himself would need to resist the urge to bypass the system when tempted to jump in directly.

One gap stood out as an opportunity. At the time, Andrew's managers weren't consistent in how they handled client requests. Turning that inconsistency into discipline wasn't just a requirement for the system to work; it was a chance for Andrew to build his muscle of leading accountability conversations that the whole business needed.

This didn't erase Andrew's Power Tension of Authority vs. Autonomy, it reframed it. He could maintain visibility without clamping down. His managers could step into real ownership without leaving him blind. For the first time, Andrew could imagine a system where accountability and trust weren't opposites, but partners.

It was only a design on paper. But even at this stage, Andrew felt the shift: a way out of firefighting, and a glimpse of the business he wanted to lead.

Step 4: Make It Real

It's one thing to sketch a promising solution. It's another to make it real in the messy, unpredictable environment of a growing business. Many ideas look brilliant on paper but collapse under the weight of daily demands. The key is not just to design well, but to test whether an idea actually works in practice.

Entrepreneurs often skip this step. Excited by the spark of a new insight, they want to leap straight to scale: building systems, rolling out technology, or training the whole team at once. The result is predictable: over-complexity, wasted energy, and the re-creation of the problems they were trying to solve.

That's why it's useful to ground every new solution in a simple mantra: **Make it work. Make it right. Make it scale.**

The sequence matters. First, you make it work: prove that a lightweight version of the idea can actually solve the core problem. Then you make it right: refine it for consistency, quality, and reliability. Only after that do you make it scale: structuring it so it can grow without collapsing.

Right now, your job is the first step: **make it work.**

Making it work is not about elegance or polish. It's about building something that is good enough for now and safe enough to try. The goal is not to get it perfect, but to learn. The faster you learn, the faster you can improve.

Thinking this way requires you to treat every move as an experiment. Instead of aiming for the final version, you create a simple test, try it in real conditions, and collect feedback. If it works, you refine. If it doesn't, you adjust. Either way, you move forward with more clarity than you had before.

In the last section, we sketched one possibility: redesign client onboarding so expectations and limits are explicit from the start. On paper, this sketch made sense across the system:

- **People:** account managers trained to confidently set expectations.
- **Process:** a standardized onboarding sequence that ensures nothing gets missed.
- **Technology:** automated welcome messages and dashboards that reinforce the agreements.
- **Knowledge:** clear documentation of what's included and what isn't.

Now comes the grounding.

In the **make it work** phase, we don't roll out a company-wide system. We start small. One account manager tries a lightweight onboarding checklist with a single new client. The script lays out what's included, what isn't, and how communication will work. After the first onboarding, we ask the client directly: Was this clear? Did anything feel missing? What would have made this smoother? That feedback shows us where the design holds up in practice and where it doesn't.

Once we've proven the idea works in a few real cases, we move to **make it right.** This is where we refine. Maybe the checklist gets reworded into friendlier, client-centered language. Maybe we adjust the order of the conversation so expectations are set earlier. We test it with more clients, across more managers, and use those experiences to tighten the process. By the end of this stage, onboarding isn't fragile; it's reliable and repeatable.

Only then do we step into **make it scale.** Now we codify. The checklist becomes a standard template for all account managers. Automated welcome emails, FAQs, and dashboards reinforce the agreements. The system spreads across the team, supported by training and technology. What started as a sketch with one manager and one client has become a durable operating rhythm for the whole business.

Notice what happened here. By following the sequence, we didn't just design an elegant solution; we tested it, improved it, and built it to last. Starting small felt slower, but it actually moved us forward faster. We got early wins, we learned quickly, and we avoided the waste of building a big system that didn't actually solve the problem.

This is the deeper power of Super Choices. They don't remain sketches; they become practical, tested moves that reshape how the business works. By resisting the urge to scale too soon, we end up creating stronger systems in less time.

So here's your invitation: look back at the sketches you made. Choose one. How could you strip it down to the smallest test that's good enough for now and safe enough to try? What would you need to learn to know it's working?

Don't aim for the final version. Aim for progress. When you make it work, then make it right, and then make it scale, you not only escape firefighting; you design a business that can carry you to the altitude you're aiming for.

Andrew Makes It Real

After sketching out the possibility of moving client communications into a centralized ticketing system with clear expectations, Andrew decided to move forward.

The pilot was small by design: one client, one property manager, and a handful of properties. Andrew wanted a test that was visible enough to learn from, but contained enough to limit the risk.

Almost immediately, the upsides showed. Client requests stopped disappearing into scattered inboxes. Each ticket had a clear owner, so accountability wasn't vague. Andrew could see issues before they escalated into crises without hovering over his manager. The property manager felt clearer about priorities, and the client noticed smoother follow-up.

But the test also revealed friction. The manager sometimes slipped back into email, forgetting to log tickets. Escalation rules felt clunky, leaving a few issues in limbo. Andrew had to fight the urge to bypass the system when he spotted something urgent. Most importantly, the pilot exposed an inconsistency: the manager hesitated to fully "own" certain tickets, a sign that accountability still needed to be built into the culture.

Instead of shelving the idea, Andrew used those bumps as design input. He and the manager tweaked the categories, simplified escalation pathways, and added a quick weekly huddle to surface stuck tickets. Each iteration made the process more intuitive and more natural to use.

As they worked out the kinks, Andrew widened the scope. More managers began using the system. Accountability conversations became part of the weekly rhythm, rather than something triggered only by failure. The system wasn't flawless, but it was working well enough that managers trusted it—and Andrew began to trust them.

The impact was noticeable on all sides. Andrew was no longer in constant firefighter mode, worried that his property managers were missing emails from clients. He had more mental space, and for the first time in years, the future didn't feel like a distant dream. His managers were clearer about their responsibilities and more confident in carrying them through. And clients saw the difference: requests were handled consistently, with fewer escalations landing on Andrew's desk.

The tension between authority and autonomy hadn't disappeared. But the ticketing system gave Andrew a way to hold both: he had visibility without micromanaging, and his managers had ownership without leaving him blind. What once felt like opposites began to operate in tandem.

The system wasn't perfect. It didn't need to be. It was enough to shift Andrew out of firefighting and into designing. Enough to give him a glimpse of the business he wanted to lead, not just the one he had to rescue.

The Pivot to High Altitude

Super Choices are the key to making the High-Altitude pivot.

The pull of the Low-Altitude Cycle doesn't disappear with the awareness of your Power Tension or the clarity of a Tension Map. Insight alone is not enough; without grounded action, your system keeps producing what it was designed to produce.

A Super Choice takes the clarity you've already built and turns it into momentum. Instead of solving the last crisis or trying to perfect the impossible balance between opposing forces, you design a new way of working that holds both sides together. Super Choices are the mechanism that transforms awareness into action and action into progress.

The result is movement that feels purposeful rather than exhausting.

Even beyond grounded action, Super Choices are a shift in the foundational context of how you and your business operate. Each Super Choice reinforces the High-Altitude Spiral by supporting you to reframe your Power Tension as a design challenge instead of an emotional burden or impossible choice.

By creating designs that honor both sides of your Power Tension, you embed intentionality into your leadership and into the systems of your business. You move from being the operator at the center of every problem to the architect of a new operating rhythm. Step by step, choice by choice, your business becomes easier to lead and more capable of sustaining itself.

In the next chapter, we'll take this further. You'll learn how to engage your team in this process so that your Super Choices don't live in your head or depend entirely on you. You'll see how to lead these conversations in a way that builds clarity, commitment, and real ownership.

CHAPTER 6

Step 4 – Catalyze Action Through Ownership

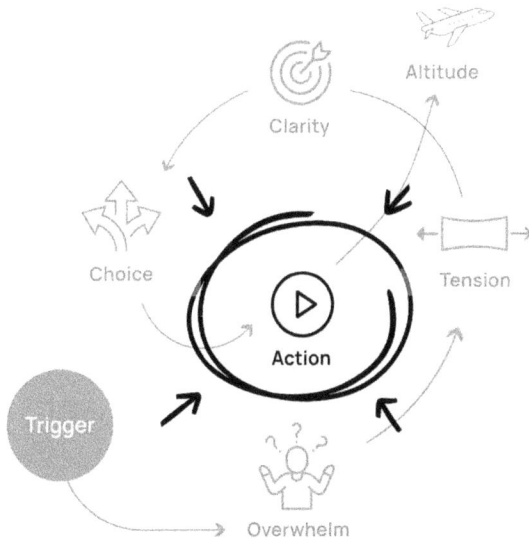

The High-Altitude Spiral: Action

"The purpose of knowledge is action, not knowledge."
— Aristotle

Michael's Story

Michael built PDQ Auto Parts on scrappiness and adaptability. In the early years, he thrived by bending processes, saying yes to custom orders, and finding clever workarounds when suppliers or systems fell short. That flexibility became his edge, fueling growth and helping him build a $25M aftermarket auto-parts company from scratch.

As the business grew, so did fragility. Inconsistency led to costly mistakes and orders slipped through the cracks. Customers started to demand reliability over improvisation. Michael and his leadership team faced a hard truth: without standardization, they couldn't keep growing.

So they did the hard work. They doubled down on systems, locked in processes, and committed to efficiency and consistency as the backbone of scale. They invested in quality and even got industry certifications.

It worked. The revenue grew, margin stabilized, and the company grew stronger and more predictable.

Now, though, Michael feels the shadow side of that decision pressing in. Standardization brought scale, but it came at the cost of agility. When high-value opportunities come in—custom parts, niche markets, strategic partnerships—the team hesitates. "That's not how we do things," they say. The structure that once gave the business stability now leaves it rigid, unable to seize possibilities that could define the future.

One moment crystallized the pain for Michael: a well-known performance parts reseller approached his company with a custom request for a high-margin part. Even though it wasn't a large order, it could have opened doors to an entirely new distribution channel.

When the proposal hit his team, the debate dragged on. Operations resisted disrupting production schedules, growth-oriented leaders pushed for the opportunity, and no decision came quickly enough. By the time they were ready to move, the customer had already gone to a competitor. For Michael, it was proof that the company's hard-won standardization now came with a steep cost: missed opportunities he could see but couldn't act on.

Michael isn't naïve to the dynamics at play. He's already done the work this book has guided you through. He's named his Power Tension: Standardization vs. Flexibility. He's mapped the upsides and downsides with his team, and the picture is clear: the business is leaning heavily into standardization. He's even pushed himself to design Super Choices, strategies that could preserve the efficiencies of scale while carving out space for innovation. On the whiteboard, the solutions make sense. In planning sessions, they look like the future.

In practice? Nothing sticks. His leadership team is entrenched. The operators cling to standardization, worried that deviation will collapse hard-won stability. The growth-oriented leaders push for flexibility, only to watch their ideas stall or fizzle. When Michael tries to bridge the gap himself—bringing integrated solutions for the team to run with—he finds they rarely gain traction. The team nods in agreement, but when the meeting ends, execution reverts to the longstanding pattern.

"I feel like I'm trying to captain a boat where no one is working the sails," he says. "I can see the future, but I can't get the team to move with me."

The reality is that the company is strong, well-run, profitable, and reliable. But Michael knows that without a way to unlock shared ownership, they'll stay stuck. The future he envisions—incorporating AI and new manufacturing technologies, innovating quickly, and disrupting the industry—depends on breaking free of this resistance.

That's where this chapter comes in: learning how to catalyze ownership with your team.

What Is Resistance?

In the last chapter, we explored how to design Super Choices—decisions that integrate the best of both sides of a tension. We presented the process in an idealized form: clarity emerges, we create the path forward, and momentum follows. That's useful as a teaching tool, but the transition from idea to action is rarely that smooth.

In real life, moving from insight to implementation is messy. What looks clear on the whiteboard can dissolve when it meets the complex dynamics of a real organization. Ideas that feel exciting in strategy sessions often stall under the pressure of day-to-day operations. This isn't a sign of failure; it's simply how business works.

Here's why: change almost always evokes resistance. Any attempt to shift habits, roles, or structures disrupts equilibrium. Even when the change is positive, it unsettles people. Most don't experience change as opportunity; they experience it as threat.

This is where a different lens helps. I have learned that resistance isn't an obstacle to crush; it's just energy in the system that's trying to maintain balance in the face of disruption. When people resist, they aren't usually being lazy, obstinate, or difficult. They're doing their best to protect something they value.

Neuroscience backs this up. David Rock's **SCARF model**, a framework developed by the NeuroLeadership Institute[5], shows that our brains respond to social situations much like physical ones. We move toward rewards and away from threats.

There are five domains that trigger these instinctive reactions:

- **Status**: our relative importance to others.
- **Certainty**: our ability to predict the future.
- **Autonomy**: our sense of control over events.
- **Relatedness**: our sense of safety and belonging with others.
- **Fairness**: our perception that exchanges are just and equitable.

Whenever one of these domains feels threatened, resistance surfaces. Not because people are trying to be difficult, but because their nervous system is wired to defend against threats.

Look at your team through this lens and you'll see it everywhere. The operator who clings to standardization isn't "resisting" innovation; they're protecting **certainty**. The growth-oriented leader pushing for flexibility isn't "resisting" process; they're defending **autonomy** and **status**, wanting to be seen as someone who can move the company forward.

Here's the catch: no one ever feels like they're resisting. What they feel is that someone else is pushing forward while missing a piece of the puzzle. Resistance isn't resistance at all; it's protection.

When leaders push harder in the face of this protection, they only amplify the sense of threat. What feels to you like urgency feels to others like pressure. What you see as "driving progress" lands for them as "you don't get it." And the more you push, the more resistance you create. It's a self-reinforcing loop that stalls the change you're trying to make.

This is why so many good ideas fizzle. It's not that the idea is wrong. It's that the way it's introduced triggers threat responses across the team. People nod in meetings but drag their feet afterward. Initiatives look strong on paper but stall in execution. From the outside it can seem baffling; from the inside, it's completely predictable.

Here's the paradox: the single most common thing seasoned entrepreneurs tell me they want is a team that takes ownership because they know that ownership leads to action.

These entrepreneurs don't want to be the bottleneck. They don't want to carry it all themselves. They want leaders who think independently, who step forward, who act like owners.

And yet, time and again, entrepreneurs who crave ownership in their leadership end up creating the opposite conditions. By pushing forward with solutions, by stepping in, by leaning on control, they generate threat responses. They close the space where ownership might emerge. Teams learn to wait them out, defer, and comply instead of commit.

Ownership doesn't happen because you demand it. It doesn't even happen because you explain it well. It happens when you create the conditions where others feel safe enough to step into it. That requires easing off your drive, even when that feels like the quickest route to safety.

That's the work in front of us now—learning how to co-create with your team instead of trying to force ownership into existence.

Co-Creation Is the Gateway to Ownership

Co-creation helps you shift your team from resistance to ownership.

Co-creation is more than a leadership technique. It's a posture. It's the difference between presenting solutions for your team to adopt and building solutions with your team in real time. Instead of showing up with a finished plan and asking for buy-in, you invite your people into shaping the path forward. The distinction is subtle but profound: compliance is replaced by commitment, and resistance gives way to ownership.

Most entrepreneurs think they're co-creating when they're not. They bring an idea they've thought through, present it with enthusiasm, and then ask for feedback.

But feedback is not co-creation.

If the team senses that your mind is already made up or that it's not safe to challenge your view, they won't step in with their best thinking. They'll nod, go along, and then quietly revert to their default behaviors once the meeting ends.

True co-creation requires you to do something that most entrepreneurs find counterintuitive: you must actually let go of the pathway to the outcome that you want. You have to bring your clarity, yes, but also your uncertainty. You have to be willing to say, "I don't have this figured out yet," and mean it.

That vulnerability doesn't diminish your authority, it builds trust. It shows your team their perspective matters, that they're not just carrying out your plan but creating it with you.

And when people feel that, resistance starts to melt. Why? Because you've flipped the script. Instead of imposing change and triggering threat responses, co-creation builds relatedness:

the sense of belonging. People feel safer and resist less when they get to contribute instead of being dragged along.

This sense of belonging is one reason co-creation is often so energizing. When it's real, the room feels different. Instead of silence or surface-level agreement, you hear questions, challenges, and laughter. People build on each other's ideas. They paraphrase to make sure they've understood. They take risks in front of each other, saying things like "I don't know" or "I'm not sure that will work." And at the end, instead of just hearing, "We'll do it," you hear concrete commitments: "I'll take this piece. I'll deliver by Friday."

Of course, co-creation is not easy. It feels slower at first. You may feel pressure to move faster and the discomfort of not having all the answers. Your team may hesitate, because they're used to waiting for you. You may find yourself tempted to step back into the expert role—the one with the solutions—because that's what built your business in the first place. These are natural tensions. The key is to notice them without collapsing back into your unconscious habits.

So how do you practice co-creation in a way that leads to action? You bring a combination of transparency and curiosity to each step of the High-Altitude Framework. Here's how that works and what the dialogue might sound like for a leader navigating the tension of Client Service vs. Boundaries.

Name Your Power Tension

Share what you're observing (without prescribing).

> "I'm noticing we've been bending over backward for clients, which makes them happy. But I'm also seeing our team burning out because we're not holding boundaries. I'm not sure how to balance the two."

Invite others' perspectives openly.

Ask questions like...

- "What's your experience?"
- "I know I move with a lot of authority, but I really want to know: what are you seeing that I might be missing?"
- "Where is this showing up most clearly in your area?"

Map Your Power Tension

Reflect and connect what's emerging.

> "So what I'm hearing is that Client Services is worried about losing accounts if we push back, while Operations is worried about burnout and mistakes from over-promising. Both are real. Let's map them together."

Create Super Choices Together

Jointly design experiments.

> "If we wanted to keep clients delighted and protect our team's energy, what might that look like? What experiments could we try?"

Commit to tangible next actions with shared accountability.

> "Where do we want to test this first? Who feels like the right person to lead it? And what timeframe feels realistic to check back in?"

Notice how different this feels from the founder saying, "Here's my solution. Dave, you own it." Ownership is not assigned; it is generated. When people shape the path themselves, their commitment is intrinsic.

When you begin practicing co-creation, don't mistake the slower pace for inefficiency. Yes, it takes longer in the meeting. But it saves you enormous time (and, more importantly, energy) later by eliminating drag, resistance, and half-hearted execution. What emerges is the source of collective intelligence and tangible action. You no longer have to push the project forward; the project pulls itself forward through the team's commitment.

This is the deeper benefit of co-creation: it's not just about making better decisions. It's about building a culture where ownership lives everywhere, not just with you. A culture where ownership is developed inside a practical structure, not just expected to materialize because you asked for it. That's where freedom starts. The work moves out of your head and into your team's hands— not because you delegated harder, but because they took it up themselves. When that happens, you stop being the bottleneck. You start building lift.

Building RQ™

Most leaders want to engage their teams more deeply. They say they're committed to collaboration, but when the pressure is on, they slip back into patterns: that are the results of their conditioned tendencies: presenting polished solutions, pushing for buy-in, or tightening control. The intention is good, but without new skills, the result is the same—compliance without real ownership.

This is where the usual intelligence categories start to feel incomplete. IQ helps you solve problems. EQ helps you understand yourself, regulate your reactions, read social cues, and manage relationships.

These abilities all matter. But even a well-developed EQ doesn't automatically equip a founder to lead in the conditions of a growing business: rapid change, compressed time horizons, power asymmetries, and teams that have learned over years to defer. In that environment, the social-awareness and relationship-management aspects of EQ need a different, more deliberate translation—one built specifically for founders who need others to lead.

That translation is RQ™, your capacity to relate to others.

RQ™ isn't a competing construct. It's the operating system for scalable leadership—the practical, repeatable way you turn social awareness and relationship management into conditions where ownership consistently emerges. It shows up in how you enter a room, how you listen, how you hold tension without rushing to close it, and how you use clarity not to dominate, but to unlock contribution. RQ™ is what allows co-creation to function as more than rhetoric. It gives structure to the softer skills founders often attempt intuitively but inconsistently. High-RQ™ leaders shift the energy in a room so that others step forward. They don't just make better decisions; they build stronger teams.

In practice, RQ™ looks like a set of capacities that shape how your team experiences you. Here are some examples:

- **Cultivate relatedness**: build genuine belonging so people feel they're growing with you, not being dragged along.
- **Invite feedback and listen with compassion**: make it safe for people to share what they see—even when you disagree—and show you're attuned to the needs underneath their words.
- **Hold space for divergent views without losing direction**: let differences surface, work through them together, and keep the room anchored to what matters.
- **Use clarity to unlock contribution**: share your thinking, your uncertainties, and your constraints so others can add their best ideas.

When you practice these skills, the shift is unmistakable. Your team stops waiting for your answers. They start bringing their own well-developed thinking. They challenge each other. They carry decisions to completion because they see themselves as co-owners, not executors. Strategic decisions feel lighter because they're carried by many, not just you.

This is the deeper shift of RQ™. It transforms leadership from a one-to-many broadcast into a shared iterative process. You move from command-and-control to co-creation without losing accountability. In fact, accountability strengthens because the work no longer lives in your head alone.

RQ™ is a way of being that enables the shift from doer to leader and makes scalable leadership possible. It's this capacity that turns your clarity into collective action—so ownership shows up in others instead of bottlenecking in you.

Like any intelligence, RQ™ isn't fixed. It can be learned, practiced, and strengthened. I work directly with leaders on building these skills for the sake of building companies that can grow without trapping their founders in the center of every decision.

Michael Practices Co-Creation

In the past, Michael tried to push his team forward with ready-made solutions, only to watch momentum evaporate once the room emptied. Today he wanted to try something different. It felt unfamiliar and risky, and he wasn't sure how his team would respond. Still, he knew the existing approach wasn't working.

So instead of arriving with a polished plan, he began by naming what he saw rather than prescribing what should happen.

"We've done the hard work of building systems and standardizing," he said. "That's what let us scale, and it's made us strong. But we've also seen how that strength has limits. When high-value opportunities show up, we hesitate or miss them." He paused, then added, "I don't have this figured out yet, but I think this is the next big challenge in front of us."

At first, the room split along familiar lines. Operations leaders leaned forward, reminding the group that production schedules were already running tight and that stability was the backbone of their success. Growth-oriented leaders countered that saying no to unique requests meant leaving money and strategic relationships on the table. The tension felt like déjà vu, the same debate looping back again.

This time, Michael didn't close the gap with his own solution. He leaned into it. "Here's the question I think we need to wrestle with," he said. "How might we protect the efficiency of our production schedules while also moving fast enough to capture high-value custom opportunities?"

The phrasing shifted the energy. Instead of defending their camps, people began speaking into the shared problem. One leader noted, "If we treat custom jobs the same as everything else, they'll always lose out. They'll clog the system or just get delayed." Another responded, "But if we build a separate track, maybe we can manage them without disrupting the core."

As the conversation unfolded, a sketch of a solution emerged: a pilot "custom projects lane" that would handle only select, high-margin opportunities. It wouldn't replace the standardized core of the business—it would sit alongside it. It wasn't a grand redesign; it was a practical experiment.

Still, the group knew it wasn't that simple. The head of engineering spoke up: "We don't have enough engineering capacity for this to work. We can't just wedge custom jobs in with the same people who are already maxed on production."

Instead of disagreeing, Michael flipped it around. "You're right. For this to work, we'd need someone designated to design these quickly, either someone in-house or a contract firm." Heads nodded. It was a clear "what would have to be true" moment, the kind of practical condition that grounded the idea.

Michael noticed the difference. In the past, he would have been the one surfacing these constraints and assigning next steps. Here, the team was doing it themselves. He listened, connected dots, and made sure all perspectives were visible, but he didn't force a conclusion.

As the meeting drew to a close, Michael leaned in. "We've surfaced some good thinking here. What are some next steps we can take to move this forward? Who's willing to own that?"

There was a pause, and then Michael's operations manager spoke up. "I'll take it. Let me schedule a follow-up so we can come back with more input on what this pilot lane could look like and who might run it."

It wasn't Michael assigning a task. It was the team stepping in— and that difference mattered.

Walking out of the room, he realized what had shifted. Instead of compliance, he'd seen commitment. Instead of resistance, there was motion. For the first time, the path forward didn't depend on him pushing harder; it depended on the team building it together.

It was just a follow-up meeting. But to Michael, it signaled that ownership had begun to move from his hands into theirs. That was the only way they'd ever unlock the future he was aiming for.

The Expectation Trap

Sometimes many entrepreneurs tell me they've tried co-creation and it "doesn't work." They bring their teams into discussions, invite input, and still end up disappointed by the results. In most cases, what's really happening is that the leader is holding a vision of success they haven't communicated, an unspoken expectation that others can't meet because they don't know it exists.

An expectation is a private mental movie of how things should unfold—visible only to you—and when reality diverges from that movie, what arises isn't mild irritation; it's deep disappointment.

This is one of the hidden traps of leadership: the clearer your vision, the easier it is to forget that others haven't seen the movie you're watching. Entrepreneurs live partly in the future. We don't just imagine outcomes; we pre-experience them. The work already feels complete in our heads—the client happy, the plan obvious—but for the team, none of it exists until you articulate it. When it's not articulated and the outcome inevitably diverges, the reaction isn't just frustration at what's in front of you. It's the shock of a violated prediction.

Brains Are Prediction Machines

Your brain doesn't passively observe reality; it actively predicts it. Neuroscientists call this **predictive processing**. Your brain constantly generates models of what should happen next based on past experience, then checks incoming sensory data against those predictions.

This predictive machinery is why you can catch a ball, finish someone's sentence, or navigate your morning routine on autopilot. It's the brain's way of saving energy by betting on what's next to stay efficient and safe.

Here's where it gets tricky for leaders: Delegating triggers the same mechanism. Your brain simulates how the work will unfold: what the output will look like, when it will arrive, how the person will handle it. You experience this simulation as an expectation.

Then comes the violation. When your team member delivers something different, even if it's objectively good, your brain flags a prediction error. Neural alarms fire, cortisol rises, and suddenly you're not leading—you're acting from your conditioned tendency.

What you feel is disappointment, frustration, or even betrayal. What's actually happening is your brain's alarm system responding to violated predictions as if they were violated agreements—even when you never articulated what you expected in the first place.

For entrepreneurs, this wiring runs hot. You've built success by simulating future scenarios, spotting problems early, and acting fast. Each time that worked, your brain got rewarded. So when reality clashes with your mental model, it doesn't just sting; it feels like proof that delegation fails and control is safer.

The expectation trap isn't personal weakness; it's predictive machinery mistaking private movies for shared agreements.

The nervous system's reaction creates what I call the Expectation–Disappointment Loop, a common dynamic that keeps even seasoned entrepreneurs stuck in the Low-Altitude Cycle. It starts innocently enough: you delegate, confident you've been clear. You picture how it will unfold: the tone of the client email, the quality of the report, the timing of delivery. But when reality diverges from the mental movie, you're triggered. Disappointment floods in. And, before you can catch them, your conditioned tendencies kick in.

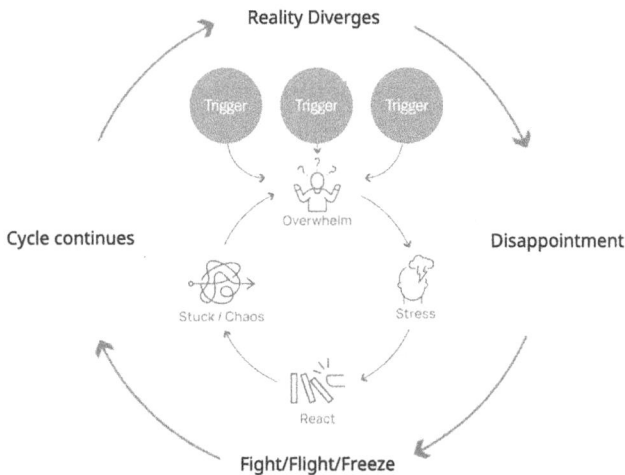

The Expectation-Disappointment Loop

Some leaders move toward the problem. That's the **fight** response. You jump in, fix it, and reassert control. "Let me just handle it." You restore order in the moment, but you also signal to the team that ownership isn't safe in their hands.

Others move away. That's the **flight** response. You pull back, decide it's easier to just do things yourself next time. You stop delegating, telling yourself you're saving time, but what you're really doing is harming trust.

Then there's the **freeze** response. You tell yourself it's fine, not worth the battle. You let the outcome slide, but inside, you're resentful and disengaged.

Each response feels different, but all of them discharge discomfort without addressing its source. Each variety of conditioned tendency perpetuates the loop. Fight breeds overcontrol. Flight breeds isolation. Freeze breeds resentment and decay. Slowly, the gap widens between the leader and the team. The company keeps moving, but trust weakens, energy drains, and true ownership never takes root.

The seduction of expectation is that it gives you the illusion of control in an unpredictable world. It feels like safety, but it's not safety; it's rigidity. What feels like holding a high bar to you lands as unspoken judgment to everyone else. You think you're leading with excellence, yet your team feels like they're failing a test they didn't know they were taking.

Over time, this dynamic erodes ownership. When expectations are unspoken, the rules of the game stay unclear. People focus on avoiding mistakes rather than creating results. Initiative drops, innovation slows, and progress depends more and more on the leader's direct involvement.

The way out begins with seeing expectation for what it is—an invisible prediction masquerading as leadership. Dropping expectations doesn't mean lowering standards. It means transforming the way you hold them. Standards are explicit and shared; expectations are silent and private. Standards create clarity; expectations create disappointment. The shift isn't to stop caring about outcomes. It's to drop your expectations and recognize that the unexpected is part of leadership. When something unexpected does happen, your job is to replace judgment with curiosity.

That's where accountability comes in. Accountability, done well, helps everyone learn from what actually happened. Instead of asking, "Why didn't this go the way I expected?" we create accountability by asking, "What happened? What did we learn? What needs to be true next time?" Accountability metabolizes disappointment into discovery. It shifts the focus from blame to learning.

That's the beginning of ownership—not the kind that's demanded, but the kind that's chosen. That shift—from expectation to accountability—helps to lift you and your team out of the Low-Altitude Cycle.

Collaborative Accountability Transforms Expectations into Ownership

Accountability is one of the most misunderstood words in leadership. For many entrepreneurs, it still carries the echo of childhood, school, and early work experiences—moments when authority meant control. "If you don't do what I want, there will be consequences." The lesson was simple: accountability is synonymous with blame; it's what happens to you when you fall short.

That model is so ingrained that even seasoned entrepreneurs unconsciously recreate it. When results fall short, they tighten the reins, impose deadlines, add pressure. But that form of accountability doesn't generate ownership; it kills it. It shifts people from contribution to compliance. It creates fear instead of focus.

True accountability is something different. It isn't punitive; it's reflective. The word itself means to give an account: to tell the story of what actually happened. Accountability, at its best, is a learning process. It's how leaders transform violated expectations into shared understanding. When we approach it this way, it stops being about fault and starts being about discovery.

Every unmet expectation carries valuable information about misalignment, assumptions, communication gaps, or system breakdowns. As we saw in the previous section, most of us experience that moment as frustration or disappointment. But if we can meet it with curiosity instead of control, that moment becomes a pivot point for growth. The question shifts from "Why didn't this happen?" to "What happened? What did we learn? What needs to be true next time?" Disappointment becomes data. Accountability, practiced this way, is how a business turns mistakes into improvement.

Traditional accountability fails because it begins from blame. "Why didn't you do this?" is less a question than an accusation. It assumes the outcome was entirely someone else's doing and that your job is to diagnose the failure. The person on the receiving end feels judged (because they are!), and naturally defends. In that instant, learning disappears.

Ironically, the harder you lean into blame, the less accountable the team becomes. They start protecting themselves from your reaction instead of addressing the problem itself.

Collaborative Accountability begins from a different premise: that every outcome is co-created. It asks, "What conditions produced this result and how did we each participate?" When we take this posture, we strengthen **relatedness**, one of the core human needs in the SCARF model. We move from "me versus you" to "us facing a problem together." That shift creates connection, which reopens curiosity. Accountability becomes connective rather than corrective, a joint inquiry into what's true and what's needed next.

There are three mutually supporting legs of Collaborative Accountability. Each one strengthens the others to turn accountability from pressure into participation.

Conversation: Begin with honest, judgment-free dialogue. Name what happened, listen to understand, share your view, and co-design the next step. Talking *with* rather than *at* converts violated expectations into learning and builds trust.

Cadence: Build rhythm through regular check-ins and reflections. A steady cadence turns accountability from a reaction to a habit and normalizes reflection, alignment, and shared learning.

Care and Compassion: Lead from care, *especially* when results disappoint. Approach conversations with compassion and the assumption that others are showing up to do their best. This keeps connection intact so people feel safe owning mistakes and learning from them. Care turns accountability into growth instead of blame.

Together, these three practices create the conditions where ownership takes root, generates action, and accountability becomes a shared act of improvement.

The Accountability Conversation

When our expectations are violated—a deadline missed or a project not advanced as promised—instead of being caught in our conditioned tendencies of fight, flight, or freeze, we can enter into an accountability conversation. The **accountability conversation** uses curiosity to create connection.

Here's the structure[6]:

Step 1. Introduce the issue without judgment.
Start by naming what you've observed, using neutral language that focuses on facts rather than evaluations. Avoid blame, sarcasm, or emotional charge. The goal is to signal safety: this is a conversation, not a confrontation. Keep your tone even and your body language open. This sets the conditions for genuine dialogue.

Step 2. Ask questions, listen, and empathize.
Invite the other person to share their view of what happened. Listen fully without interrupting or rushing to conclusions. Demonstrate empathy by reflecting both content and emotion: acknowledge the pressure, constraints, or intentions that shaped their choices. Ask follow-up questions that show curiosity, such as "And what else?" or "What made that challenging?" The aim is to understand the whole picture before adding your own perspective.

Step 3. Share your own concerns clearly.
Once you've listened, share your perspective in the open, non-defensive tone of co-creation. Frame your concerns as inputs to a shared design challenge, not as verdicts. Explain what matters to you, what constraints you're holding, and why. Speak from clarity, not control. Your goal is to bring your priorities into view so they can be considered alongside others.

Step 4. Summarize both perspectives.

Before moving forward, recap what you've heard and what you've shared. Summarizing aligns understanding and prevents assumption. Name the key themes, points of agreement, and real tensions that remain. Check for accuracy and invite correction or addition. This step transforms a one-way exchange into a shared map of reality that both parties recognize.

Step 5. Co-design the next step.

With shared understanding in place, shift to action by asking, "How might we move forward?" Generate solutions together that respect the concerns on both sides. Focus on what's possible now rather than rehashing what went wrong. Commit to clear next actions and decide how you'll revisit progress. This final step turns accountability into motion by converting insight into improvement and learning into ownership.

Each step reinforces shared responsibility. You're not excusing mistakes or lowering the bar; you're building the capacity to meet it together. Ownership grows because people feel part of the solution rather than the subject of scrutiny.

The Accountability Conversation in Practice

Let's imagine that the founder of a mid-sized manufacturing firm and her operations director had co-created a Super Choice to test a regional pilot—an experiment designed to explore new markets without overextending the core plant. The plan was sound, but two months later, the pilot had stalled. Instead of reacting with frustration or pulling back, the founder turned to the Accountability Conversation to revisit the commitment.

Step 1. Introduce the issue without judgment.
"I've noticed our regional pilot hasn't gained traction," she began. "Can we take a look at what's getting in the way?"

Step 2. Listen and empathize.
The operations director explained that production demands at the main facility had intensified, leaving little capacity for the pilot. The founder acknowledged the reality and reflected it back: "It sounds like the core business has been absorbing more than we anticipated, and that's stretched the team thin."

Step 3. Share your own concerns clearly.
She then shared her perspective in the Super Choices frame: "The thing is, we created this pilot to expand our options beyond the core. I don't want our need for stability to make us risk-averse."

Step 4. Summarize both perspectives.
She paused to make the tension explicit: "You're holding the need to protect operations and meet current demand, and I'm holding the need to keep our growth initiatives alive. Both matter."

Step 5. Co-design the next step.
Finally, she asked, "How might we move forward?" Together they agreed to narrow the pilot's scope to one client instead of three and to review staffing capacity before restarting.

The outcome was modest but meaningful. The conversation restored alignment without blame and turned a stalled initiative into a learning moment.

Accountability became a structured way to stay connected in pursuit of the larger goal.

The Cadence of Accountability

When something goes unexpectedly—a commitment missed, a result that falls short—the accountability conversation gives you a way to respond with curiosity rather than control. It helps you metabolize disappointment into learning and restore alignment in real time. But even the most skillful accountability conversation is reactive by nature: it happens after something has already gone off course.

To build a company that learns continuously, rather than only when something breaks, you need something more—a **cadence of accountability.** This is the proactive counterpart to the accountability conversation. Instead of waiting for surprises to trigger reflection, you create regular, predictable moments to look back, learn, and realign before things drift too far. Cadence turns accountability from a corrective act into a rhythm of growth.

What you're really doing is normalizing reflection. When reflection becomes habitual, accountability stops being about blame and starts being about awareness. It weaves learning into the operating system of your business so improvement becomes routine, not reactive.

At its simplest, the cadence of accountability is a recurring space—weekly, biweekly, or after key events—where the team steps back to reflect. The structure is deliberately lightweight and easy to sustain. It centers on three deceptively simple questions:

1. What went well?
2. What didn't go well?
3. What do we want to try next time?

That's it. Fifteen to thirty minutes. No slide decks, no postmortem theater. Just a candid conversation about what happened and what you'll do differently. When asked with genuine curiosity and a sense of ownership, these questions shift attention from fault-finding to pattern-finding. They reinforce the truth that progress is iterative and that every project, success, and setback is one more data point in building a smarter, stronger system.

Rhythm builds resilience and capacity. As you and your team reflect regularly, you strengthen your ability to stay steady when things don't go as planned. Instead of reacting to breakdowns with blame or urgency, you learn to meet them with curiosity and coherence. As a result, you and your team learn to move skillfully through uncertainty without relying on perfect foresight.

Your role as founder is to model this rhythm and make it a standard by showing how to hold the space with curiosity, then ensuring the practice spreads until it becomes the company's heartbeat.

This rhythm works at any scale. A leadership team might hold a short Friday review to reflect on the week's progress and plan what to try next. After completing a client project or campaign, a quick retrospective locks in what worked before moving on. Even concluding a project call with a two-minute "what worked/what didn't" conversation about the call itself builds the same muscle.

This rhythm also distributes leadership. When accountability lives in cadence rather than hierarchy, everyone becomes responsible for learning. Reflection stops being something that happens at the top and starts being something that happens everywhere. That's how a company becomes generative and able to stretch toward ambitious goals without waiting for top-down direction. Problems still happen, but they don't derail you. Teams still stumble, but they recover quickly because the system learns without your constant intervention.

That's the real payoff of a cadence of accountability: breakdowns are part of the game, fuel for your ascent rather than a barrier to it.

The Power of Celebration

Leaders (and often their teams) tend to skip over what went well. The human impulse is to jump straight to what's broken, what's late, and what needs fixing. But accountability is about seeing the full picture of performance, including the wins you might otherwise rush past.

Celebration is not fluff. It's data. When you deliberately notice what worked, you uncover patterns worth repeating. You see the moves, decisions, and collaborations that produced strong results, so they can be reinforced and replicated.

Celebration also does something data alone cannot—it builds connection. When teams take a moment to acknowledge progress, big or small, they remember that they're creating something together. Shared recognition turns individual effort into collective achievement. It rekindles the sense of us that gets lost when everyone is heads-down chasing goals.

In this way, celebration strengthens relatedness. It reinforces capability, confidence, and belonging all at once. Teams who feel seen for what's working show up more fully for the next challenge. Success stops feeling like luck and starts feeling like something you're building together.

Celebration restores balance. Most organizations unconsciously train a "negativity bias," where the only time reflection happens is when something fails. Over time, that bias erodes initiative. People learn to speak up only when there's a problem, not when there's progress.

Real accountability includes both sides. It means learning equally from what went well and what didn't go so well. When teams build that muscle, reflection stops being an avenue for criticism and becomes a source of momentum and collaborative energy.

Care and Compassion Are the Foundation of Collaborative Accountability

Collaborative Accountability grows from care. Not the kind of care that rushes in to comfort or rescue, but the more centered form that says, I see you, I'm with you, and I want you to succeed. Care is the stance from which all real collaboration grows. It creates the sense of being accompanied, not managed. When people feel that kind of care, they stop performing and start participating. They take creative risks. They bring more of themselves forward. They trust that mistakes can be discussed rather than hidden. Care, in this sense, isn't sentimental, it's structural. It's what holds the human system of a company together.

Without care, accountability collapses into control. When care disappears, leaders start trying to enforce outcomes instead of cultivating ownership. They tighten deadlines, increase scrutiny, or add more reporting—anything to drive compliance. It looks like accountability, but it's really coercion. Coercion works, briefly. People do what they must to stay safe, but their energy turns defensive. They protect instead of contribute. They say yes but mean maybe. What gets lost is both motivation and truth. Without care, accountability conversations become rituals of self-protection rather than moments of shared learning.

Compassion is the ability to connect with another's suffering. When accompanied by a genuine desire to help, compassion is what sustains care when things get hard. It's the steadiness to stay open and connected when disappointment enters the room. Every leader faces that moment: a promise broken, a project missed, a result that didn't meet expectations. Compassion is what keeps you from turning away or closing off. It's the willingness to stay in contact, to keep listening, to see the person in front of you as more than the mistake they made. That steadiness communicates safety: You can tell me the truth. It won't cost you belonging. When people trust that they're safe, accountability stops feeling like exposure and starts feeling like growth. They no longer hide behind partial explanations or defensiveness; they step into responsibility because it feels safe to do so.

This is what creates the foundation for creative risk-taking. When compassion undergirds accountability, teams know they can stretch without being punished for imperfection. Experiments, candid reflection, and course correction all become possible because people trust that their worth isn't on the line. Compassion frees people to reach higher because they're not expending energy on self-protection. Compassion builds the kind of resilience that control can never produce.

The way leaders express compassion is through curiosity and openness. Curiosity asks; openness receives. Curiosity is the act of leaning in—What was happening for you there? What were you seeing that I wasn't? Openness is the discipline of letting the answer land, even when it's not what you hoped to hear. Together they create a space where truth can emerge without fear. This kind of listening is rigorous. It seeks to understand before deciding, to learn before judging. In that space, accountability becomes dialogue. Both people grow wiser because both are willing to be changed by what they hear.

Care begins the relationship; compassion sustains it. One opens the door, the other keeps it open when stress arises. Most leaders underestimate how powerful this is. When you meet disappointment, the real measure of leadership is how deeply you connect. Correction restores performance; connection restores trust. Accountability rooted in care and compassion strengthens both. It turns the hardest conversations into moments of shared creation where the goal isn't just to fix what went wrong, but to grow together into what's next.

The Journey to Ownership

Co-Creation and Collaborative Accountability may sound "touchy-feely."

That's because they are.

They also require rigorous skills to deal with the softest and hardest part of business at once: people. Every system, process, and strategy eventually runs through the hearts and minds of human beings. When those human systems fail—when trust breaks, when communication frays, when people start protecting rather than contributing—it's because the relational fabric is weak.

Soft skills are what hold that fabric together. They are the result of your RQ™ (see the sidebar **Building RQ™ earlier in the chapter**), the backbone that turns co-creation and accountability into conditions where ownership can actually take root. They determine whether your culture can metabolize stress or whether it shatters under pressure. They decide whether truth moves freely through your organization or gets filtered by fear. You can have brilliant strategy and flawless execution on paper, but without care, curiosity, and compassion, those systems seize up when real life intrudes. In the end, it's not the "hard" skills that sustain a company's growth; it's the capacity of its people to stay connected through change.

That's why soft skills are business critical. They're the infrastructure of adaptability. The ability to co-create, hold accountability conversations, listen without defensiveness, and navigate disappointment without blame—these are the muscles that propel growth. They don't replace performance discipline; they make it possible. Without them, excellence becomes brittle. With them, it becomes repeatable.

This is the paradox many entrepreneurs miss. The harder the environment, the more the soft skills matter. As complexity increases, technical fixes yield diminishing returns, and the bottleneck becomes relational. The leaders who scale aren't the ones who master more control; they're the ones who can create coherence in the midst of uncertainty.

When you run your organization through the joint practices of Co-Creation and Collaborative Accountability, everything doesn't have to go perfectly. You loosen your grip to experiment. You trust the process for learning and repair. The team knows how to navigate imperfection together.

That's what creates a culture of creative risk-taking: people stretch further, experiment more boldly, and recover faster because they know the system can hold them. That's what ultimately leads to ownership.

Entrepreneurs sometimes worry that leadership anchored in care, curiosity, and compassion means lowering the bar. It can sound like a recipe for indulgence, the kind of "soft stuff" that lets underperformance linger or excuses poor behavior in the name of understanding. Many founders have scars from that mistake: the employee they held onto too long, the partnership they tried to "coach through" when what was really needed was a clean ending. They learned the hard way that kindness without clarity corrodes culture.

This fear misses the point. Compassion isn't the opposite of strength; it's what allows strength to land cleanly. To lead with compassion is not to avoid hard calls; it's to make them without resentment or reactivity. Care means staying present enough to see reality clearly and act decisively when alignment is gone.

Not everyone will thrive in this kind of system. Some people prefer direction. Sometimes, no amount of dialogue will correct what turns out to be a fundamental mismatch between an employee and their role. That's okay.

When practiced well, compassion gives you the steadiness to hold accountability without aggression, and to part ways with someone in a way that preserves dignity—for them, and for you.

Co-Creation and Collaborative Accountability create ownership, generate action, and break the Low-Altitude Cycle. Your company becomes a living system that learns from itself. As it does, your own freedom expands and you no longer need perfection to feel safe.

You have a process.
You have trust.
You have ownership.
You have altitude.

Compassionate Presence

Most leaders underestimate how much their own nervous systems get in the way of listening. On paper, compassionate presence sounds simple: stay open, stay curious, and stay connected. But in practice, it's one of the hardest things to do. When the pressure rises, even seasoned entrepreneurs slip into conditioned tendencies that protect rather than connect.

These tendencies are actually smart survival strategies. But left unchecked, they block the awareness that co-creation and accountability depend on.

The most common blockers to compassionate presence come from well-worn internal scripts:

- **The need to look good and be right** – You focus on performing rather than perceiving, filling the space with your certainty instead of others' perspectives.
- **The fear of not knowing** – You rush toward solutions as if speed can protect you from uncertainty.
- **The urgency to get things done** – You convince yourself that listening is a luxury rather than a lever for clarity.
- **The avoidance of vulnerability** – You resist not being in control, steering conversations toward the familiar and shutting down the parts of you most capable of connection.

Giving in to these impulses feels like safety, but it comes at the cost of progress.

When you operate from these states, your body tightens, your breath shortens, and your field of awareness narrows. You stop listening and start reacting. Dialogue becomes debate, accountability becomes critique, and even your best intentions to align, clarify, and drive progress land as pressure. Compassionate presence evaporates not because you don't care, but because you're working from a place of threat.

The work isn't to override these reactions through willpower; it's to develop the capacity to notice and recover faster. Compassionate presence begins when you realize that awareness itself is an act of leadership. The shift first happens in the body through breath, grounding, and deliberate slowing. When you can feel your own reactivity without acting from it, you create the space where new understanding can emerge. That space is the birthplace of ownership.

Compassionate presence is not soft. It's the discipline that allows you to meet tension without tightening and to hold others' perspectives without losing your center. Without it, collaboration collapses into control. With it, you create the conditions where ownership and trust can actually take root.

Michael's Journey

Over the past few months, Michael has been noticing a quieter kind of progress—the kind that doesn't announce itself in metrics or milestones, but in how he moves through his days.

When we first met, his attention was on structure: building systems, setting standards, scaling execution. Those things still matter, but now he sees that the harder, deeper work is relational. It's the shift from performance management to partnership, compliance to collaboration, and control to care.

He says it plainly: "I used to think the problem was ownership. But really, it was safety. People weren't taking ownership because they didn't yet feel safe to try, get it wrong, or take a risk. I had to learn how to make that safety real."

That realization didn't arrive all at once. His early efforts at co-creation didn't go as expected. Meetings went long. Ideas fizzled. Momentum stalled. His unconscious reflex was to step in, tighten the reins, and take over. "I thought I was helping," he admits, "but what I was really doing was taking the work back."

Those moments became the turning point. Michael began to see that accountability and care weren't opposites. They could be built together—not through control, but through collaboration.

With the support of coaching, he started experimenting with a new approach. Slower conversations. More listening. More curiosity. When tensions surfaced, he began naming what was working before naming what wasn't. The first few times, it felt awkward, almost performative. But gradually, something shifted. People leaned in instead of shutting down. They began to share what they were actually seeing, not what they thought he wanted to hear.

In one of our later sessions, he reflected on the surprise of it. "It wasn't about lowering expectations," he said. "It was about raising trust."

Michael built that trust through collaborative accountability. Michael joined clarity with care, and people started owning the outcome because they believed their contribution mattered.

As the team learned and built trust, something tangible began to change. The Super Choice we explored earlier—the custom projects lane they had co-designed months earlier—finally came to life. Instead of stalling in endless revisions, it gained momentum. Because they had built capacity, they were able to take on two new custom projects. Margins came in stronger than expected and Michael is now exploring deeper partnerships with those clients.

The real win was cultural: people followed through without being pushed. Progress stopped being something Michael had to enforce; it flowed naturally from collaborative ownership.

He noticed it in the tone of meetings: fewer updates, more problem-solving. In the rhythm of execution: more initiative, less reactivity. In the way his team spoke to each other: more honesty, less defensiveness.

Michael still catches himself wanting to jump in with the familiar surge of urgency when something feels off. Then, on a good day, he remembers that his job isn't to fix the issue. It's to strengthen the way people are working—to help them see the tension for themselves.

And when things inevitably wobble, as they do, he doesn't frame it as failure anymore.

He put it best in one of our closing conversations:

> "This isn't a finish line. It's a practice. I'll probably always have the instinct to step in and take back control because it's part of how I'm wired. But now I notice it faster and recover sooner. I've learned that showing care isn't being soft; it's providing structure. And collaborative accountability... that's the bridge. That's what keeps us moving forward."

The real story of his growth is how he expanded into his own leadership. Over time, he developed a presence that is steady, discerning, and deeply human. He now moves through challenges with a kind of internal spaciousness, meeting tension without being overwhelmed by it.

"Honestly," he said, "I don't think this work ever ends. I'm good with that. Because working this way, with care and real collaboration feels lighter. We're still ambitious, still moving forward, still growing, but it doesn't feel like pushing anymore. It feels like flow. That's new for me."

He looked down for a moment before finishing.

"If this is what leadership feels like—steady, human, connected—then I'm exactly where I need to be."

CHAPTER 7

Putting It into Practice

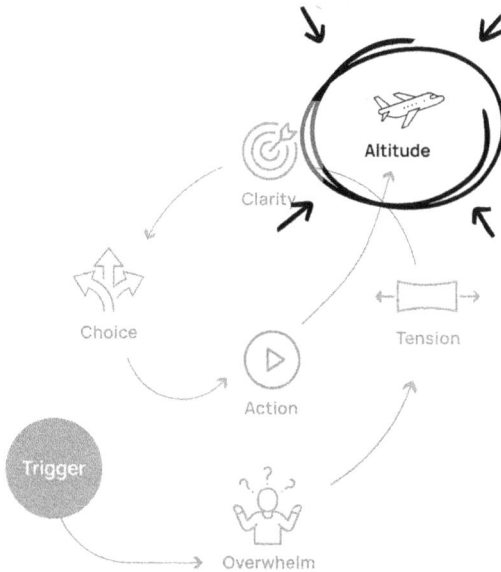

The High-Altitude Spiral: Altitude

"Until you make the unconscious conscious, it will direct your life and you will call it fate."

— Carl Jung

The Gap Between Action and Altitude

When we last left Priya, the CEO of Wow! Foods, she had begun to breathe again. Working through the High-Altitude Framework™ had given her space. She'd started mapping tensions instead of rushing into fixes, inviting her team to own more of the process, and even ending her days at a reasonable hour. A few months later, the difference was noticeable. Meetings ran smoother. Decisions didn't bottleneck around her. She could sense her business running on something steadier than her adrenaline.

Then came the second national account. It was the kind of news every founder dreams of—the kind that validates the sleepless nights and the risks that felt impossible to justify at the time. Priya felt a surge of pride and relief. But beneath that celebration, a familiar thought flickered: this one has to go perfectly. The more she repeated it, the smaller her newfound spaciousness became.

At first, it showed up subtly. She lingered longer in team check-ins, reopened threads she hadn't touched in weeks, and told herself she was just "keeping an eye on things." One evening, she stayed late after everyone had gone home, glancing over the week's production schedule, something her operations manager now handled entirely. Nothing looked wrong, but the batch sequence didn't feel quite right. Without thinking, she started rearranging orders in the Google Doc, telling herself she was helping things run smoother.

Half an hour later, she caught herself mid-edit. Nothing was on fire. There was no crisis demanding her intervention. The only thing pulling her back into the weeds was the reflex to protect what mattered most. In that quiet recognition, she saw the pattern: resistance wasn't loud. It was subtle, reasonable, almost responsible.

That's where the real work begins. Every entrepreneur who grows beyond their old way of leading will meet the urge to move back to comfort just as progress starts to take hold. What Priya felt wasn't failure; it was resistance announcing itself. Next, we'll explore how to recognize that signal for what it is and how to use the High-Altitude Framework™ to turn resistance back into progress.

Expect to Experience Resistance

As Priya's story shows, it's one thing to understand how ownership emerges. It's another to practice it, especially when that practice asks you to loosen your grip on the approach that once helped you succeed. Many entrepreneurs reach this point and feel a strange paradox: clarity about what needs to change and resistance to actually doing it.

You've seen the patterns. You know how control crowds out ownership, how over-delegation breeds drift, how pressure erodes co-creation. And yet, when you start to move differently—to delegate more deeply, invite more voices, or slow down enough to listen—something in you tightens.

That tightening is resistance.

In the last chapter, we explored resistance as a natural force in your organization's system—the way teams instinctively defend stability when change threatens the familiar. The same thing happens inside you. Your own inner system strives for equilibrium too. When change challenges your sense of competence, belonging, or control, your body and mind instinctively push back to preserve safety.

This is why resistance can feel confusing. It rarely announces itself as fear or avoidance. More often, it shows up wearing the mask of leadership: a subtle return to control, the need for speed, and the urge to clarify just one more time. After all, you built your business on decisiveness and follow-through. But beneath those moves, your nervous system is working hard to protect the identity that success was built upon.

You might notice yourself arriving with the answer already formed, steering conversations toward your preferred outcome, rescuing silence when others hesitate, or stepping back in just to "keep things moving." These are all sophisticated forms of resistance. They look like diligence, but they come from doubt and the part of you that wonders, If I don't do this, will it still get done right?

None of this is failure. It's physiology. The nervous system protects what it knows. Resistance isn't sabotage; it's a safety mechanism. It's trying to preserve the familiar conditions that kept you successful so far. But what once kept you safe can now keep you small.

That's why resistance often appears at the moment of progress. You start to stretch beyond the limits of your current identity—the fixer, the expert, the one who holds it all together—and your system senses danger. Even positive change can feel like loss because it asks you to relinquish certainty for possibility.

So when you feel resistance, take heart. It's merely a signal that you're evolving. The gap between knowing and doing—between intention and action—is the friction of transformation itself. Resistance arises precisely because something real is changing.

The invitation isn't to fight it or push through it. Pressure only deepens the threat response. The more you try to "fix" yourself, the more your system braces. Instead, treat resistance as information, a cue that it's time to work the practice. Each time resistance shows up, it's pointing to the edge of your growth. That's the moment to pause, breathe, and return to the High-Altitude™ framework—to map what's happening, name the tension, and reengage from awareness rather than reflex.

Resistance means something meaningful is at stake. It's proof that you're in motion. When you can meet it with curiosity instead of control, it becomes the energy that lifts you higher.

Common Blockers

Knowing what you're encountering is the first step, but resistance doesn't disappear just because you understand it. The key is to recognize the form it takes in you. Pay attention to your personal blockers, the reactive patterns that kick in when you're stressed and looking for safety.

Once you recognize these blockers, you can learn how to respond in ways that keep you moving through the High-Altitude Spiral rather than collapsing back into the habits that keep you trapped in the Low-Altitude Cycle.

Here are some common blockers and what you can do about them.

1. Holding onto Problem-Solving

"I'll just fix this; we don't have time to unpack it."

Instead of pausing for inquiry or inviting the team to explore what's really happening, urgency takes the wheel. The co-creative instinct gets replaced by motion. Solving feels decisive and action restores control. But in closing the loop too quickly, learning is lost. The system gets relief instead of progress and the pattern resets.

Subtext: If I'm not making things happen, it's not going to happen.

High-Altitude Intervention: When you notice yourself slipping into automatic problem-solving, that's your cue to turn back to the High-Altitude Framework™. The instinct to act is rarely wrong; it just needs to be redirected from fixing to seeing. The first step is to pause and map the tension before you move. Instead of asking, How do I solve this? shift the question to *What's really happening here? What's the pull beneath the surface?*

Tension Mapping breaks the spell of urgency. It turns the invisible dynamics—Speed vs. Quality, Control vs. Trust, Stability vs. Innovation—into something you can name and work with. That single act of naming converts reactivity into reflection. Once you see the opposing forces clearly, you can move deliberately rather than reflexively. You stop collapsing complexity into "a problem" and start treating it as a living system that's giving you feedback.

The pressure eases not because you've solved it, but because you've reentered awareness.

From that vantage point, you can design a Super Choice that integrates rather than overcorrects. Instead of swinging between extremes ("Do I slow down or push through?"), you create an experiment that honors both needs. You might decide, for example, to let the team own the next iteration while you set a single learning checkpoint midstream. The point isn't perfection; it's practice. Each time you slow the reflex to fix and instead map or integrate, you train your system and your team to stay in inquiry longer. Over time, that becomes your new muscle memory: action grounded in awareness and progress born from learning, not relief.

2. Holding Onto Control

"Send it to me before it goes out."

Delegation invites others to stretch; control creates a perception of safety. The intended behavior of trusting the process gives way to guarding outcomes. What looks like diligence is often the nervous system's way of tightening the reins when uncertainty rises. Every time the leader takes work back, the organization learns that ownership isn't real.

Subtext: Letting go means things will fail catastrophically.

High-Altitude Intervention: The first step in loosening control isn't to delegate harder; it's to map the tension underneath the impulse to take things back. What's really being managed isn't the task; it's the fear of what might happen if you let go. By mapping your Power Tension, you begin to see the hidden cost of control.

Paying attention to the perceived downsides forces that truth into view: each "quick fix" that restores order also teaches the team that ownership is temporary. Each reassurance you give yourself erodes the capacity you're trying to build in others. And, often, the worst case you fear turns out to be manageable.

When you see that clearly, control stops feeling like protection and starts looking like a ceiling on your and your team's growth. That recognition alone creates space for a new choice.

From that awareness, you can design **Super Choices** that let you practice trust without abandoning accountability. Instead of swinging from over-control to over-freedom, you create safe experiments, bounded spaces where delegation can succeed or fail without existential risk.

For example: "I'll review the first two drafts, then step back completely for the third," or "We'll pilot this new approval process on one client before applying it company-wide."

These experiments integrate both sides of the tension. They preserve the sense of safety your nervous system craves while demonstrating that shared ownership can, in fact, produce strong outcomes. Over time, each successful experiment rewires the belief that letting go means catastrophe. You learn that safety doesn't come from control; it comes from clarity, trust, and the structure of the process itself.

3. Being the Expert

"Let me just weigh in."

True co-creation asks for curiosity; expertise substitutes certainty. An entrepreneur might intend to facilitate discovery, but instead fills the space with answers. Influence is regained, ambiguity recedes, and the conversation flattens. The system orbits around the one who knows, not the question that matters.

Subtext: If I don't know, I'm worthless.

High-Altitude Intervention: Leaning into curiosity begins with noticing the reflex to explain. For seasoned founders, expertise has long been a source of value and safety—the way you've proven competence, earned trust, and kept things moving. But when leadership becomes a platform for answers, it narrows the field of discovery. A focus on catalyzing ownership reopens that field. It's the deliberate act of trading certainty for awareness, of shifting from "What should they know?" to "What might we learn together?"

This mindset doesn't diminish your authority; it refines it. In the High-Altitude Framework™, curiosity is not passive listening. It's active orientation toward what's alive in the system—the tensions, assumptions, and unspoken fears shaping behavior. When you lead with inquiry, you model the ownership you want your team to take: engaged, humble, and learning in public. Over time, that posture transforms culture more than any single insight ever could.

Practically, curiosity means entering each conversation imagining that the most valuable information is the piece you don't yet have. Instead of asserting what's true, ask what's missing. Replace statements of fact with invitations to explore: "What are we not seeing yet?" "What would have to be true for that to work?" "What are the risks we're underestimating?" These questions expand leadership. They turn meetings into laboratories of shared thinking rather than stages for individual performance.

The paradox is that curiosity, while it feels slower, accelerates ownership. When people sense your genuine interest in their perspective, they step forward with greater responsibility. They move from compliance to contribution because the space allows them to matter. Over time, your influence deepens, not through answers, but through the quality of attention you bring. That's the essence of High-Altitude leadership: presence over performance, inquiry over expertise, discovery over display.

4. Prioritizing Consensus Over Co-Creation

"Let's get more input before we decide."

Co-creation and consensus both invite participation, but they serve different masters. Consensus seeks comfort; co-creation seeks clarity. In consensus, the goal is agreement: to eliminate tension so everyone feels at ease. In co-creation, the goal is alignment: to surface tension so the best path forward becomes clear. Consensus smooths difference; co-creation works with it. The first prioritizes harmony in the moment and the second prioritizes progress over time.

Even when a leader intends participatory clarity, consensus can sneak in as comfort management. It trades decisive co-creation for extended conversation. Agreement becomes the metric of safety, not alignment on purpose. The system drifts toward sameness, mistaking peace for progress.

Subtext: It's a big problem if people are angry with me.

High-Altitude Intervention: The way out of consensus is structured co-creation. Map your tensions to make the real forces in play visible. Start meetings by presenting the opposing forces underneath competing perspectives: Efficiency vs. Exploration, Stability vs. Growth, Quality vs. Speed.

When those forces stay implicit, they sound like disagreements; when they're made explicit, they become shared material to work with. Each polarity on the map shows the legitimate pull of both sides. Instead of asking, "What do we agree on?" you ask, "What's the tension we're managing here?" This small shift reframes differences as data. The team sees that discomfort isn't a breakdown; it's the source of progress. Over time, mapping tensions normalizes productive friction. People stop defending positions and start owning the conversation together.

In the moment, when you sense yourself drifting toward consensus—softening your stance to keep the peace or scanning the room for nods—pause and name what's happening. You might say, "It feels like we're trying to agree, but we haven't named what's really pulling on us yet." Then use the Tension Map to locate it. Is the group leaning too far toward control? Too far toward speed? This move grounds the conversation in the system, not the personalities. You're teaching your team that alignment doesn't mean everyone feels comfortable; it means everyone is clear about what's in play. Each time you do this, you strengthen the muscle of co-creation and your ability to stay with a tension long enough for ownership to emerge.

5. Sitting on the Sidelines

"I'll come back when I'm ready."

This pattern shows up when a leader wants to co-create but can't yet tolerate being seen in the messy middle of learning. They analyze, plan, and observe, wanting to "get it right" before engaging. It's not about perfecting the outcome, but perfecting the self before participation. Planning becomes a form of self-protection, a way to appear thoughtful while avoiding the vulnerability of real-time experimentation. The process looks careful, but in truth, it's stalled.

Subtext: If I look foolish, people won't follow me anymore.

High-Altitude Intervention: When you catch yourself sitting on the sidelines—planning, analyzing, waiting until you feel ready—the High-Altitude move is to map what's actually happening inside. What looks like hesitation is usually a live tension between two healthy impulses: the desire to be thoughtful and the desire to be seen as competent. The more you privilege the first, the more you protect the second. Mapping this tension externalizes the conflict. Instead of being you versus your courage, it becomes two legitimate needs in dialogue: the need for preparedness and the need for participation. Seeing it on paper restores perspective. You stop confusing prudence with paralysis.

Once the tension is visible, treat it like any other in your business: clarify what each side protects, and what each side makes possible. The instinct to be prepared protects quality and foresight; the move to step in now creates connection and momentum. Both matter. Your work isn't to choose one, but to experiment at the edge where they meet.

This is where the idea of "good enough for now, safe enough to try," which we explore as part of Super Choices, comes in. Give yourself a defined container—a time, a meeting, a specific conversation—where you'll step forward imperfectly and let learning happen in public. The constraint turns vulnerability into structure. It shifts the question from "Am I ready?" to "What will I learn when I show up anyway?"

When you show up this way, you model something far more powerful than mastery. You model permission. You show your team that leadership isn't the absence of uncertainty; it's the willingness to explore it. Each time you act before you feel ready, you strengthen your capacity to hold discomfort without retreating. That's the essence of High-Altitude leadership—not flawless control, but steady presence in the messy middle where growth actually occurs.

The Underlying Pattern

These patterns aren't failures of leadership; they're the echoes of past success. Each one once generated results (even if the result was successfully coping with trauma), which is why they still feel so convincing now. The more we rely on them, the less room we have to lead. The work now isn't to reject them, but to see them clearly enough and to reach for the High-Altitude Framework™ to soften their grip on us.

These are some of the most common blockers you're likely to encounter, but they're not the only ones. Your own version may look quieter, subtler, or shaped by the unique pressures of your business. Even if you don't see yourself exactly in these examples, the same principles still apply. What matters isn't whether your pattern has been named, but that you can recognize when you've slipped into the Low-Altitude Cycle and know how to find your way out.

The High-Altitude Framework™ meets you wherever you are. Its practices—naming your Power Tension, mapping it, making Super Choices, and catalyzing co-creating with your team—work not because they target a single pattern, but because they help you see and shape whatever pattern you're in.

Priya Closes the Gap

The next morning, Priya felt the familiar tug of vigilance that used to send her diving back into the details. The new account was ramping up, orders were growing, and the week ahead looked demanding. Her instinct whispered that she should "just make sure" everything was aligned. But this time, she stopped. She recognized the pattern: the pull to protect the business by taking it all back into her hands. Instead of opening the production sheet, she reached for her notebook. She had learned enough through the High-Altitude Framework™ to know this was the moment to pause, not push.

So Priya began to map what was really happening. She realized that this issue was really about and the tension between **control** and **trust**. So she mapped it:

Looking at the map, she could see her own pattern clearly. When pressure rose, she swung hard toward control for safety even though it trapped her in dependency. Trust still felt unfamiliar, but she could finally see that it wasn't recklessness; it was an investment in future stability. Mapping the tension made the tradeoffs visible. Control brought comfort but capped capacity, while trust invited risk but built resilience.

That awareness opened the door for a Super Choice. Rather than tightening her grip or stepping back completely, Priya named what was happening and turned it into a learning experiment. She shared her Tension Map with her ops lead, who immediately got what was happening.

Her ops lead admitted that she, too, had been caught in her own tension between working independently and reaching out for support. As the pace and pressure increased, she craved a sounding board but didn't want to bother Priya with trivial details.

So they went to work with a How Might We Question. How might we create visibility and support without bringing Priya back into the weeds and disempowering the ops lead?

Together they designed a simple rhythm, a weekly retrospective where they would each bring reflections: what went well, what didn't, and what they wanted to try next. It was a small, deliberate move that gracefully navigated Priya's need for safety with her commitment to shared ownership—a Super Choice that turned awareness into practice. It was an easy thing to try and something they could refine over time.

For Priya, the urge to intervene didn't vanish, but it softened. The next time she wanted to step in, she noticed it instead of acting on it. She could see now that her discomfort wasn't an enemy to overcome—it was a signal, marking the edge of her growth. By mapping, naming, and designing from that awareness, she'd converted reactivity into reflection. The High-Altitude Framework™ was a living practice that turned anxiety into alignment.

This is what leveraging the framework looks like in real life. It doesn't erase resistance; it transforms it. The moment Priya paused, mapped, and reengaged, she turned tension into progress. That's the power of practice. When awareness replaces reflex, leadership begins to breathe again. In the next section, we'll explore what it means to participate in that work: how to stay with the discomfort of growth long enough for transformation to take root.

Participate in This Work

Each step of the High-Altitude Framework™ and each case study is an invitation to look at what's happening in your business right now. It's an opportunity to see the benefits and the costs of how you're operating. But being a passive consumer of the framework isn't enough. You have to participate in the work.

Participation means engaging with this process: naming your tensions, mapping them, and exploring your conditioned tendencies. Every time you put language to a tension, you raise your altitude. Every time you see your own conditioned tendencies clearly, you loosen their hold. Every time you work openly with your team, you generate curiosity and build trust.

The High-Altitude Framework™ can be used for major strategic decisions at the core of your business. As Priya's story shows, it can also be used in the day-to-day. It's a way of thinking and a way of being that centers your and your team's ongoing growth and development. It creates an upward spiral that can take you wherever you want to go.

Awareness is the first step. Continued practice supports you to keep your insights relevant and generative. The pull of unconscious habits is strong, especially when the pace picks up or uncertainty returns. You can't outthink those reflexes; you have to practice your way into new ones.

That's the intention behind **elevate**, a monthly gathering I host for High-Altitude Entrepreneurs to keep working these tools in real time, together. I'll share more about how to join in the conclusion, but for now, remember: lasting change doesn't come from what you know; it comes from what you practice.

The High-Altitude Framework™ in Practice

My client, Laurel Parks, the co-founder and COO of Houston Pump and Gear, wrote to me with a story of how she was using the High-Altitude Framework™ in real time. It's such a simple yet powerful example, I wanted to share it in her own words:

A quintessential example of my Power Tension, Strategic Focus vs. Urgency, came up today. I am at the office with a few key strategic objectives lined up for completion.

About an hour after I arrived, my business partner called with an emergency lead.

The customer needed a six-foot pump shaft with a keyway manufactured before Monday. I knew I could make it happen, call suppliers, pay the break-in fees, line up materials, and coordinate with the machinists. But all of that would take at least three to four hours and completely derail my focus for the day.

So I asked a few simple questions:

Who's the client? What are they willing to pay?

I knew I could do all that, but it would cost us progress.

In the end, we realized the amount the customer was willing to pay just wasn't worth the trade-off. Pause. Respond differently.

The reason I love this example and wanted to share it with you is it demonstrates just how powerful a pause can be. The pause Laurel took changed not just her decision that day, but also her relationship to urgency itself. She shifted her perspective, stepped out of the weeds, and reshaped her context.

CONCLUSION

Creating What's Next

"The most powerful leadership tool you have
is your own example."
— John Wooden

At this point, you've done something few entrepreneurs ever do. You've stepped off the treadmill of urgency long enough to see the patterns running beneath your business and your leadership. You've looked straight at the habits that once built your success and recognized how, unexamined, they began to limit it. In seeing clearly, you've stopped being at the mercy of your business and started designing it instead. You've learned to see tension not as failure but as information, as the raw material of growth.

The work has been both practical and personal. You've mapped business tensions that clarified what once felt like chaos. You've experimented with new ways of responding—pausing where you used to push, asking where you used to tell, and creating space for others to step forward. Maybe you've already felt the moment of recognition when you catch yourself in an old reflex and choose differently. It's not dramatic, but it's profound. That single breath of awareness reshapes everything that follows. The difference isn't just what you do; it's who you're being while you do it.

That shift ripples outward. When you lead from awareness, your team feels it. Pressure eases. Conversations open. Ownership starts to emerge. The system around you starts to reflect the steadiness you've cultivated within yourself. This is what it means to gain altitude: not to rise above the work, but to spiral up within it. You've begun to build a business that mirrors the freedom you've been chasing all along.

That freedom doesn't stop at the office door. As the business steadies, space opens to think, breathe, and reconnect with the parts of your life that have been waiting for you. Emails stop hijacking evenings. Weekends start to feel like weekends again. You find yourself more present with your family, more patient in conversation, and more curious in friendship. Ideas return—not the frantic kind born of pressure, but the quiet, generative ones that show up when your nervous system finally trusts it's safe to rest. The same clarity that's reshaping your business begins to shape your life.

While this work can seem subtle, its effects compound into dramatic shifts. I know this because I have seen how entrepreneurs who engage with the High-Altitude Framework™ shift.

Jim slowed his urgency long enough to let his team lead, and within months, escalations and rework dropped by a third while calm became contagious.

Rose replaced reaction with reflection, created the space to build a relationship with a vendor that saved her hundreds of thousands of dollars each year, and stopped chasing low-margin work that robbed her focus.

Andrew shifted from control to co-creation; meetings slowed down, decisions decentralized, and mid-level leaders had an onramp to running the business with him.

Michael transformed growth from pressure to partnership, doubling custom wins without adding chaos.

And Priya learned to meet pressure with presence, transforming her reflex to control into a practice of trust. As she did, her team's ownership expanded, operations steadied, and growth no longer came at the cost of her peace of mind.

None of them did it by hustling harder. Instead, they did it by seeing the system they'd built and choosing to redesign it. They all changed, not through massive effort, but by getting curious about their own contributions to their context. And in doing so they translated awareness into choice.

In engaging with this book, so have you.

The more clearly you see your own tendencies, the more freedom you have to reshape them.

You're taking on the deeper work of entrepreneurship, the practice of noticing, again and again, that every system, conversation, and result begins in you.

Sustaining the Journey

Freedom isn't a finish line.

It's a rhythm and a way of meeting what's hard with awareness instead of reactivity.

You'll still feel the pull toward urgency, toward fixing, toward the unconscious reflexes that once made you successful. That's natural.

But each time you pause, map, and choose differently, you reclaim authorship. You remind yourself that you're not trapped inside the systems you've built; you're the one shaping them.

That's what's at stake now. Not just higher margins or calmer meetings, but changing the way you lead through what's hard. The way you listen instead of solving. The way you hold two truths when one would be easier.

The upside of this isn't just about ease and growth in your business. It's the expansion of freedom, however you define it: taking time off for a yoga retreat with your best friends from college, nurturing a deeper relationship with your spouse, coaching your kid's lacrosse team and never missing a game, or boarding a flight to Thailand for a once-in-a-lifetime family adventure.

Each moment of choice is a small act of creation, a way of bringing more alignment, integrity, and freedom into the system around you.

Again, insight alone won't change how you lead. These principles only come alive through practice.

That's why **elevate** is essential.

elevate is the practice field where High-Altitude Entrepreneurs turn awareness into embodiment—where the framework becomes reflex and replaces habitual responses.

It's an online community where we put the High-Altitude Framework™ **into practice** together each month: mapping live tensions, designing Super Choices, learning from each other and turning theory into results.

You can't think your way into leading differently. You have to practice your way there—again and again, in community, until new habits take hold and freedom becomes your default operating mode.

That's what **elevate** is for.

It's not a continuation of the book, it's where the work becomes real.

Where you retrain your reflexes, build new muscle memory, and turn altitude into lived experience. It's clarity you can feel in your team, your decisions, and your days.

If you're ready to practice leadership at altitude, I invite you to enroll at no charge.

clearfieldleadership.com/elevate

This is the work of a High-Altitude Entrepreneur—to integrate what you've learned until it becomes how you lead.

Keep practicing. Keep co-creating. Keep climbing.

Here's to you—leading from altitude.

APPENDIX A

Common Tensions

Using this Appendix: Your Field Manual for Navigating Tensions

This is your cheat sheet. Whether you're mid-read or deep in the trenches months later, this list is here to help you spot the tensions shaping your business right now.

Each one of these tensions is a pattern I've seen again and again in my coaching work among founders like you, with real teams, real stakes, and real complexity.

Some will jump out immediately. Others might name something you've felt but haven't articulated yet.

Don't overthink it. Use this list like a field manual:

- If you're mapping your Power Tension, scan for the one that best fits your current challenge.
- If you're stuck in a swirl or firefighting, flip through to pattern match.

- If you're coaching your team, use this to guide a conversation that gets below the surface.

Not every tension here will apply. But one might shift how you see your situation—and that can change everything.

Common Tensions Entrepreneurs Face

Leadership & Decision-Making

- **Control vs. Delegation** – Direct everything yourself or trust your team to own it?
- **Speed vs. Thoroughness** – Move fast to seize momentum or slow down to get it right?
- **Vision vs. Execution** – Set direction or drive daily outcomes?
- **Gut vs. Data** – Trust instinct or run the numbers?
- **Confidence vs. Humility** – Hold the line or invite challenge?

Growth & Strategy

- **Profit Now vs. Invest for Later** – Maximize short-term gains or reinvest for scale?
- **Innovation vs. Optimization** – Disrupt what's working or refine it?
- **Expand vs. Focus** – Enter new markets or double down on your core?
- **Short-Term Wins vs. Long-Term Health** – Hit today's numbers or play the long game?

- **Customization vs. Scalability** – Tailor for clients or standardize for efficiency?

Team & Culture

- **Accountability vs. Autonomy** – Set clear ownership or give space to lead?
- **Transparency vs. Discretion** – Share openly or filter to reduce noise?
- **Inclusivity vs. Selectivity** – Open the door wide or raise the bar?
- **Process vs. Flexibility** – Stick to the playbook or adapt in real time?
- **Work-Life Integration vs. Separation** – Blend work and life or draw firmer lines?

Client & Market

- **Volume vs. Value** – Serve many or go deep with fewer?
- **Bespoke vs. Standard** – Personalize or systematize?
- **Service vs. Boundaries** – Go the extra mile or protect your margins?
- **Consistency vs. Evolution** – Keep brand tight or evolve as you grow?
- **Client Focus vs. Founder Sanity** – Please the client or preserve your health?

Personal Growth

- **Adaptability vs. Stability** – Stay nimble or lock in structure?
- **Speed vs. Sustainability** – Work fast or build to last?
- **Self-Reliance vs. Support** – Do it yourself or ask for help?
- **Freedom vs. Responsibility** – Chase optionality or commit fully?
- **Ambition vs. Contentment** – Push for more or rest in what you've built?

ACKNOWLEDGEMENTS

This book was born from the tension of simultaneously running a business and launching a creative project—crafted in the in-between moments, refined in the crucible of feedback, and shaped by the wisdom and generosity of many.

To my incredible team, Kristen and Rahne: your care, candor, and commitment made this work not just possible, but joyful. You held the space for this project to unfold while keeping our business going and our clients well-served.

To my friend and *Meltdown* co-author András Tilcsik for the inspiration and insight you've provided through the years. To my friends in Dobbs Ferry, NY, and my partner in development, Illya Bomash. To Roger L. Martin, who has offered intellectual inspiration over the years, brought a critical eye to my work, and generously offered to review an early version of this manuscript.

To my coach and mentor, Ben Laws: thank you for seeing what I was really trying to do before I could name it. Your insight and encouragement anchored my clarity again and again.

To my peers at Strategic Coach: your questions, stories, and strategic honesty sharpened my thinking more than you know.

To the many beta readers—including Alejandra Moreno, Alex Prindle, Alisa Fiddes, Alison Whitmire, Allie Kazalski, Anthony Luna, Ben Laws, Brad Coulter, Brian Dixon, Cathey Davis, Cecile Haarseth, Chad Rassmusson, Charlie Wallace, Chris DellaFranco, Clint Sievers, Dan Low, Dan Sullivan, David Jones, Frank Clearfield, Gary Wichansky, Geoff Deane, Jeff Becker, Jeff Benton, Josh Saterlee, Julian Torres, Kari Brunson Wright, Kavan Peterson, Landen Goodnight, Lane Taylor, Larry Scammell, Laurel Parks, Laurie Ehrlich, Leighton Harris, Liam Brown, Maggie Dalzell, Mark Cooper, Matthew Stein, Michael Bungay Stanier, Mike Honderich, Misha Glouberman, Nate Secor, Nathan Gregory, Nicole Martin, Oscar Velasco-Schmitz, Paul Reinitz, Renae Lattey, Rob Levin, Sam Murphy, Steve Gordon, Thaddeus Shrader, Tiffany Dehan, Tim Hammond, Walter Wilson, and Xylon Saltzman—who generously shared what landed, what didn't, and what was just confusing: thank you for helping me write a better, braver book.

To the brilliant marketing and product development team at Rogue, Kristi Capurso and Juliana Farrell: thank you for building a brand that could hold this work. Your sharp copy and strategic clarity made the book not just readable, but resonant. To the team at Ushi Ink, Ushi Patel and Montana Fisher-Shotton, the vision for this book came alive through the colors and imagery you artfully designed. Thank you.

To Amy MacClain, who walked this journey with me in different ways and provided support, thought partnership, and incisive feedback.

To my teachers, those I have worked with directly, and those who have guided me through their writings: Ali Schultz, Amba Gale, Andrea Ovans, Ben Schick, Diana Chapman, Gay Hendricks, Jerry Colonna, Jim Dethmer, Kaley Klemp, Lynne Twist, Michael Bungay Stanier, Misha Glouberman, Pamela Fry, Parker Palmer, Peter Block, Peter Senge, Renya Larson, Steve Zimmer, Sharona Halpern, Stuart Simon, and Tim McCavitt.

Thanks to Paul Reinitz for his insights about copyright and creativity in a world of Generative AI. And to Jordyn Palmer for helping to keep my life (mostly) on the rails.

To Bruce Bookman Shihan, Melissa Pittman-Fisher, and my community at Tenzan Aikido who keep me centered and grounded. Onegaishimasu.

To my parents, who provided love, support, and the precise conditions I needed to become who I am. To Brien and Linnéa, whose friendship and support help me become a better parent and a better human. To Ellen, thank you for teaching me how love heals and for being an amazing partner on this life journey. Finally, to Torvald and Sören, whose presence in my life reminds me why freedom really matters.

A Note About Names

As a coach, my conversations with clients are always confidential. Trust is the foundation of this work. At the same time, many of the entrepreneurs I work with have been incredibly generous in allowing me to draw on their experiences to support this book and the transformation it offers.

I have navigated this tension by creating composites that capture key details of their stories. My goal in doing so is twofold: to honor the leaders who have opened their journeys for the benefit of others and to ensure confidentiality. Every example reflects real entrepreneurial struggles and breakthroughs—insights that can help you navigate your own path with more clarity, freedom, and confidence.

A NOTE ON COPYRIGHT, CRAFT, AND COLLABORATION

This book was shaped not only by long walks, sticky notes, and deep conversations—but also with the help of Generative AI writing tools.

I used these tools as a creative partner throughout the process: to synthesize reader feedback into sharper drafts, to pressure-test composite client stories, to anonymize coaching dialogues, and to explore stylistic options that pushed the writing forward.

Every sentence in this book reflects my judgment and intent. But I want to acknowledge the role of these tools in making the process more dynamic, iterative, and rigorous.

They didn't replace the work. They enhanced it—just as any good collaborator would.

REFERENCES

1   Martin, Roger. 2021. "Strategy & Integrative Thinking." *Medium* (blog). July 16, 2021. https://rogermartin.medium.com/strategy-integrative-thinking-96ac0769709b.

2   This is a form of what management guru Roger Martin calls "integrative thinking." Roger writes about his own process for integrative thinking with co-author Jennifer Riel in their brilliant book, Creating Great Choices. Riel, Jennifer, and Roger L. Martin. 2017. *Creating Great Choices: A Leader's Guide to Integrative Thinking*. Harvard Business Press.

3   Abbott, Martin L., and Michael T. Fisher. 2009. *The Art of Scalability: Scalable Web Architecture, Processes, and Organizations for the Modern Enterprise*. Pearson Education.

4   Lafley, A. G., and Roger L. Martin. *Playing to Win: How Strategy Really Works*. Harvard Business Press, 2013. Google Books.

5   Rock, David. 2008. "SCARF: A Brain-Based Model for Collaborating with and Influencing Others." *NeuroLeadership Journal* 1 (1): 44–52.

6   This method is adopted from the work of Dr. Ross Greene and Roger Schwarz. See e.g., Greene, Ross. 2016. *Raising Human Beings*. Scribner and Schwarz, Roger. 2013. *Eight Behaviors for Smarter Teams*.